A Motivational Approach to Selling

A
Motivational
Approach
to
Selling

James F. Evered

amacom

A Division of American Management Associations

Library of Congress Cataloging in Publication Data

Evered, James F.
    A motivational approach to selling.

    Includes index.
    1. Selling.   I. Title.
HF5438.25.E93   658.8'5   81-69364
ISBN 0-8144-5738-X   AACR2

First Printing

To
Joanne, Kristi, Erich, and Jane—
    my reasons for living

Contents

Prologue

I offer my sincere congratulations to the fine men and women who have what it takes to be successful salespeople in today's world. They are a special breed, set apart from the ordinary. Our national economy would come to a standstill if it weren't for them. The sales representative is the main link between the world of production and the world of consumption. It is the sales representative who moves all the goods from the mine to the mill, from the field to the factory, from the warehouse to the retail store, and from the shelf to the consumer.

Selling is one of the most rewarding, challenging, interesting, and diversified of all careers. Selling is not just a job, but an exciting profession marked by men and women who have acquired a vast knowledge of people, human behavior, products, and skills. It is recognized as the very lifeline of our economic system.

Unfortunately, too many people equate selling with some of the more questionable practices they have run into. Some think only of door-to-door selling, others relate to a high-pressure used car salesman they have encountered, and still others think only of the uninspired clerk behind the counter who mutters, "May I help you?" It is an unfair indictment of the selling profession to identify it solely with these examples.

Without salespeople, we would not have the modern conveniences we enjoy in America today. The ideas all had to be *sold:* someone had to be sold on manufacturing them, someone had to be sold on marketing them, someone had to be sold on advertising them and getting them into your hands. The raw materials had to be sold to the manufacturer. So did the equipment the manufacturer uses.

How do your physician and druggist learn about new drugs? A sales representative presents the story to them. How does the clothing store owner learn about the latest fashions to stock? A sales representative tells him. How does the clothing manufacturer learn about newly developed fabrics? A sales representative tells him. If you happen to be sitting in a chair as you read this, think how many salespeople were responsible for that chair's being there. Someone sold the lumber or steel to the manufacturer. Someone sold him the screws, the rivets, the tubular aluminum, the springs, and the fabric. Someone sold him the machinery required to turn those materials into a finished chair. The manufacturer's sales representative sold the chair to the distributor, the distributor sold it to the furniture store, and the furniture store sold it to you.

All the goods and services produced in America today would be worthless without salespeople to move them. Manufacturers and other businessmen are totally dependent upon salespeople to bring them new and innovative ideas, new materials, new products, new equipment, new ways of doing business, new shipping methods, new business control forms, and new security methods to protect their businesses. Salespeople make it happen.

Sadly, many people have a negative attitude toward selling and toward salespeople. This attitude is really unfair to the profession, but it exists. This negative attitude has been caused by previous encounters with a few unsavory salespeople, those who use high-pressure tactics, who are dishonest, who misrepresent their product or use shame psychology to get people to buy. Sure, we've all seen this kind of person, but this type is a definite minority. The day of the loud-mouthed, backslapping, cigar-smoking peddler who speaks with forked tongue is gone. Unfortunately, that stereotype persists in the minds of many people. The vast majority of people in selling today are honest, hardworking, and sincere, with a genuine concern for the people who buy their products. They realize that the products and services they sell help solve people's problems, and they have no reason to feel guilty about selling them.

A service station salesman did you a favor when he spotted that balding, bulging tire, and sold you a new one. He may have saved your life. He did you a favor when he sold you a new fan belt and saved you an expensive service call out on the highway. Think of the grateful families whose children were able to get a college education because an insurance salesman sold them a program of financial security; or the widow who is able to live out her life in comfort because someone sold her late husband adequate financial coverage.

Selling is not something you do *to* a person. Selling is something you do *for* a person. Selling isn't talking people into buying something they don't need. It is persuading them to buy something they *do* need. Unless you honestly and sincerely believe the customer will be better off with your product or service, you have no moral right to sell it. Would you feel the slightest guilt in selling safety glasses to a lathe operator? Of course not. Would you feel ashamed to sell a fire extinguisher to a farmer who is beyond the reach of the fire department? Of course not. Don't you think you would be doing that farmer a favor?

In a broad sense, almost everyone is selling. It may be a tangible product such as automobiles, plastic pipe, toys, books, clothing, pharmaceuticals, or electronic calculators. Or it may be an intangible service such as insurance programs, advertising, or investment programs. Your physician is selling a service, just as the architect, the attorney, the engineer, the accountant, and the school teacher. You are selling your services in whatever job you now hold. Your company is paying for your time, your work, and your intelligence. If you stop and think about it, it's difficult to find anyone who is not, in some way, selling.

WHY SELLING?

People go into selling for a variety of reasons. For some, it's the challenge; for others, it's strictly higher income; still others, because they enjoy doing it. Perhaps it's the element of freedom, being on their own, traveling, meeting people, or an opportunity to use their personal skills. Some see the selling job as a stepping-stone into management within a company. Others consider sales work as an excellent career with a potential of high earnings. Many who entered selling as a stepping-stone found it so enjoyable and rewarding they decided to make a career of it and gave up their aspirations toward management.

Many corporate executives today came up through the sales ranks. In selling, they learned how to deal with people, how to plan, and how to organize their activities. Sales gave them valuable experience that helped them become successful top executives. The potential for a person who can sell is almost unlimited.

Even during the Great Depression, few top salespeople were seen in the soup lines. They were working, because the few businesses and companies that continued operating were completely dependent upon salespeople to keep their products moving. They had to have salespeople to survive. Salespeople are needed at all times, regardless of the economic conditions of our country. The goods must keep moving, and it's the salespeople who move them. The ability to sell is probably the best financial security you could own. You will always be in demand.

Regardless of your reasons for selecting selling as a career, you face a future of challenging excitement and practically unlimited rewards. But not everything will come easily. Desire alone isn't enough. To be a successful professional salesperson requires a vast amount of knowledge, unlimited drive and ambition, a lot of hard work, rigid self-discipline, and the necessary skills to influence others.

Unfortunately, not everyone who chooses selling as a career succeeds. Many are unwilling to work hard enough; some lack the necessary persistence; some don't have the personal characteristics required; others are not willing to study, train, and develop the necessary self-discipline to become successful.

Requires Training

Good salespeople aren't *born*—they're trained or developed. Sure, our personal qualities, desires, ambitions, mannerisms, and knowledge are the result of our background, education, and experience. As a result, many have already acquired some of the characteristics of a successful salesperson to a degree. But to succeed in selling will require the development of many qualities to a high degree. This requires training and self-development.

Some new salespeople fail because they never overcome their initial fears. Fear is the greatest enemy of a new salesperson, and fear is the embryo of failure. Some of the most common are fears of:

Inadequacy in a new job or profession
Lack of acceptance
Inability to communicate with strangers
Possibility of groping or faltering in conversation
Loss of self-confidence in a strange situation
Economic failure
Criticism
Rejection
Failure

These fears can be overcome by effective study, training, and a disciplined application of the knowledge and selling skills gained.

Importance of Attitude

Before we actually get into the sales techniques and skills, let's lay a little groundwork to get us pointed in the right direction. Call it attitude if you want, but it's mighty important. I mean your attitude toward what you are doing.

If you were to ask any salesman, "What's the first thing you have to do to succeed in selling?" he'd say, "Sell yourself!" I would agree, but my definition of "sell yourself" is probably different from yours or his. To me, "sell yourself" means more than shining your shoes, wearing business attire, smiling, grooming yourself daily, shaking hands, being friendly with the customer, and so forth. Those things are important. But to me "sell yourself" means getting yourself wholeheartedly sold on what you are doing.

As I mentioned earlier, selling is not something you do *to* people; it's something you do *for* people. You have no right to sell a product unless you sincerely believe the customer will be better off for having bought it. On the other hand, if you sincerely believe the customer will be better off buying from you, then it is your responsibility to do everything possible to help the person buy it. The customer who buys elsewhere may get less for his investment than you could have offered him. Learning ways to help your customer buy wisely is one of the objectives of this book.

Whether you are a veteran in the field of selling or are relatively new to the profession, this book is designed to lead you toward higher income and a higher degree of success. I have tried to bring you the very best and most successful techniques of thousands of successful salespeople in twenty-one countries with whom I have worked during the past two decades.

If there is any criterion we might follow to help ensure our success in selling, it is the pattern of known successful sales-people. Establishing a pattern of "thinking" and "conduct" of a successful and professional salesperson will give us a pattern to follow, which experience has shown leads to a successful and enjoyable career in selling.

To some degree my style of writing may violate literary protocol, because I will be writing primarily in the first person. This book is written *for* you; therefore, I am writing it *to* you.

By no means is the field of selling dominated by men. Nor have I found any substantial difference in performance between men and women in selling. I am a firm proponent of women in selling. The term *salesman,* which appears occasionally, is used strictly in a generic sense in this book. No offense should be taken either to the use of masculine pronouns to avoid clumsy sentences.

This book is written primarily for three types of people. First is the veteran professional who seeks new ideas and techniques to improve productivity and, at the same time, wants to reinforce or sharpen existing practices. Second, the man or woman who is new to the field and wants to reach a high level of productivity as quickly as possible. Finally, this book is written for those who have thought about entering the sales field but continue to feel discouraged about their own talents as salespersons. This is an unfortunate waste of potential in many people.

I have never found that the ability to sell is limited to a "gifted few." Some avoid selling because of negative attitudes toward the profession. Others have convinced themselves they do not have the qualities necessary to become successful at selling. They should not be so quick to dismiss a profitable opportunity without making an in-depth examination of just what selling is and what it takes to be successful at it.

I am thoroughly convinced the world is full of capable people who could be highly successful at selling if they would only stop convincing themselves otherwise. There is no mystique to selling. It is a matter of learning the disciplines and techniques of influencing others, of helping others see and understand their problems, and showing them a logical way of solving those problems. Even the personality characteristics of successful salespeople can be developed. This book can be of enormous help to any individual who wants to develop the necessary techniques, disciplines, and personality.

Sales Basics Are Universal

What you sell, that is, the product or service, may be quite different from what others sell, but the fundamentals of influencing the buyer are universal. This is true whether you are selling an insurance policy to a family, light fixtures to a hardware store customer, a computer to a corporation, a manufactured home to a retired couple, or a 200,000-ton tanker load of polyethylene plastic resin to a manufacturing plant in Singapore. Everything about the product may be radically different, but the basic fundamentals of influencing the customer to buy are the same.

You will find the approach presented in this book quite different from others you have read. I have always believed in *effective simplification* of the selling process. Everything I bring you has been validated. Every technique works. The book could have been twice the size had I included a lot of sales theory, but I don't think that is what you want. The procedures I have presented make sense. You will be able to learn them in minimum time and will be able to apply them successfully. My primary concern is in helping you succeed.

Since the material is approached from a new and different standpoint, I merely ask that you maintain an open mind throughout the book. I will challenge, perhaps, some of the conventional methods you may have learned in the past; however, I challenge them only because I feel there is a better way. By the time you reach the end of the book, I am confident you will agree.

Throughout this book little emphasis will be placed on

specific product knowledge. Although product knowledge is essential for anyone in selling, I have found salespeople rarely fail because they don't know the product.

The problem lies not in a lack of product knowledge but in a lack of understanding of the selling *process*. It is essential that a sales interview follow a logical sequence of items which must be achieved one by one. This is the *process* of selling. The successful achievement of each step in the process is dependent upon the achievement of those preceding.

The book will teach you the selling process in a logical and understandable way. You will then be able to apply your specific product knowledge to the process. Proper application of accurate product knowledge, in a valid process, leads to more successful selling. That is my objective.

1

A Motivational Approach

In order to be successful at selling, it is essential to understand the basic concepts of motivation. After all, in any selling situation our objective is to motivate the customer to buy. If a salesperson approaches the sales situation from a motivational standpoint, the progressive steps required to produce a sale become crystal clear. Moreover, a motivational approach can substantially reduce the time required to bring a sale to a close.

A motivational approach, however, may require some changes in your thinking regarding more conventional techniques that have been used in selling for years. My more than twenty years' experience in training sales personnel has caused me to question seriously the validity of several sales techniques that have been taught, accepted, and practiced with varying degrees of success. I believe too much selling time is wasted, either in doing the same things harder and harder, or in doing the wrong things better and better.

I have always found that one of the chief marks of a top salesperson is the constant search for a better way of doing something. I don't mean cuter ways or trickier ways, but more intelligent ways. Don't misunderstand me. I am not saying that selling skills that have been taught for years are all hogwash. Nothing could be farther from the truth. But I do question some of the techniques, and I question the justification behind some of them.

Hazard of Mediocrity

Further, I believe that the insistence on clinging doggedly to certain techniques and procedures in selling has caused us to accept a certain level of sales mediocrity. One needs only to analyze the sales/call ratio of a small group of salespeople in a single organization to validate this acceptance. Why will the sales/call ratios be so different among these people when all have been subjected to the same training, all are dealing with the same product, the same pricing structure, in comparable territories and under similar, if not identical, variables?

The typical salesperson or sales manager will quickly rationalize the difference with such statements as these: "When you're dealing with people . . . !" or "Territories are so different you just can't . . . !" I feel that salespeople and sales managers have hidden behind these rationalizations too long. They serve only too well as justification for mediocrity. Sure, there are differences in people and differences in territories. However, those variables are not great enough to justify the broad spectrum of sales/call ratios we usually find.

Another factor that contributes to the problem is the personal independence exercised by salespeople, independence which is frequently not curbed. There are countless people in sales work who continually refuse to follow the sales techniques they were taught. Apparently they elect not to believe that the skills are valid or that they have a high frequency of success. This is one of the most frustrating problems for sales managers. Sales training programs historically have stressed "here's how to do it" and have neglected the "here's *why* it works." As a result, many people in selling were never really sold on the procedures.

Series of Goals in the Process

A motivational approach to selling will establish the *why* as well as the *how*. The purpose or objective of motivational selling is not to produce a sale, but to guide the customer through a series of actions which will *result* in a sale. That concept may be difficult for you to grasp, but it is extremely significant. Without a firm understanding of this concept you may find most of your selling effort completely off target. The sale itself is the culmination of a process during which several significant goals are achieved. Although it may sound like heresy, the achievement of those various goals is more important to the salesperson than the resulting sale.

If you enter a selling situation in which your mind is on the ultimate sale, you are already off target and a sale is less likely to result. Anticipation of the sale will certainly hinder the process. Fear of losing the sale will almost certainly cause you to lose it. If you are preoccupied with the sale, the potential commission, or the loss you may incur if you don't get the sale, then you cannot properly concentrate on the series of objectives that must be met if the sale is to occur. There is a definite series of objectives which must be achieved, one by one, if a sale is to result. A motivational approach to selling will keep your focus on each of the individual objectives until they have been met—in sequence. If each is met in order, the odds of reaching the overall goal, the sale, will be substantially increased.

This book is written for both the new salesperson and the experienced one who is willing to take an open-minded approach to perhaps a different way of influencing a buyer, is willing to lay aside (not discard) conventional thinking, and wants to approach the sales situation with a fresh perspective. The early part of the material will make little reference to selling. It will concentrate on a few of the basics of motivation. Later, those basics will be applied directly to the sales situation. If we are going to motivate a customer to buy, we must understand how motivation works.

2

Fundamentals
of
Motivation

If we reduce motivation to its simplest terms, it is the effort through which we produce a behavior in another person. The ultimate behavior we wish to produce in a customer, of course, is the signing of the order. Therefore, it is essential that we understand how to generate or produce certain behaviors in others. Many feel that learning to motivate others means learning to be some kind of amateur psychologist. Not so. We have been motivating others since the day we were born. Any time you are influencing another person you are motivating.

It is, however, almost impossible to study the fundamentals of motivation without examining the contributions made over the years by some of the leading behavioral scientists. For years, professionals have studied human behavior to learn why people behave as they do, and to learn how we can influence the behavior of others in a positive and productive way. In this book we will examine those contributions most directly related to influencing the behavior of a customer, behavior that will help lead to a sale.

ROLE OF BEHAVIOR

Reduced to its simplest term, behavior is a means to a result and, in turn, our behavior is shaped by the result it produces.

BEHAVIOR ⟶ RESULT

Everything we do, no matter how irrational or sensible it may seem at the time, is done because of the result or outcome we expect it to produce for us. When a behavior occurs, one of three things will happen:

A positive result or outcome which we find favorable
A negative result or outcome which we find unfavorable
No result at all

In order to make the concept easier to understand, we will begin building a model for behavioral results, as seen in Figure 1.

At this point it is appropriate to refer to the contribution of one of the earlier behaviorists, E. L. Thorndike. In his "Law of Effect" Thorndike said, in essence, "Behavior which tends to lead to reward (positive result) tends to be repeated. Behavior which tends not to lead to reward (no result) or which tends to lead to punishment (negative result) tends not to be repeated." * In other words, when a behavior occurs and we find the result favorable to us, the behavior is strengthened and will tend to be repeated. The behavioral result is illustrated in Figure 2.

Figure 1. Behavior—a means to a result.

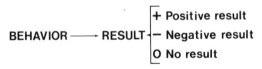

---

* E.L. Thorndike, *Human Nature and the Social Order.* New York: Macmillan, 1940.

Figure 2. Results shape our behavior.

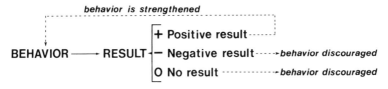

Thorndike's concept is fundamental. It is the very basis by which we train a puppy or a child. When we teach a puppy a new trick, we reward proper performance with a treat, perhaps a cookie, a bite of meat, or just a pat on the head. The puppy finds the outcome (result) favorable and repeats the performance in order to gain another reward. The behavior is reinforced or strengthened.

When a child begins taking those first few steps, he or she is encouraged to repeat or continue the performance through positive reinforcement, an encouraging remark, a smile, a hug, or a kiss. The child finds the result favorable and tends to repeat or continue the activity. The behavior is reinforced or strengthened.

Conversely, when the outcome or result is found to be unfavorable (negative result), the behavior will be discouraged and tends not to be repeated. In our example of training the puppy, let's assume that instead of rewarding him for performing the new trick we severely scolded or spanked the puppy. Getting him to perform again would be extremely difficult. The puppy is smart enough to know that performance which leads to a scolding or spanking isn't worth repeating. As Dr. Robert Mager says, "People learn to avoid the things they're hit with." *

Again, this is all fundamental, but it is essential that we understand it if we are to motivate others. We tend to respond

* R.F. Mager, and P. Pipe, *Analyzing Performance Problems.* Belmont, Calif.: Fearon Publishers, 1970.

favorably to those things we find rewarding or positive and to those things which give us a sense of self-satisfaction. Most people agree readily with the concepts that positive results tend to reinforce behavior and that negative results tend to discourage or stop behavior.

Another concept presented by Thorndike is the most overlooked: behavior which tends not to lead to reward (no result) tends not to be repeated. In other words, if a behavior occurs and nothing happens, it has the same effect as a negative result—that is, the behavior tends not to be repeated. The individual takes a "who cares?" attitude. The behavior is an exercise in futility. There's nothing in it for the individual. Any good supervisor knows that a job well done must be rewarded in some way. If no reward is forthcoming, the behavior tends not to be repeated. This is basic to behavior management.

SELECTING BEHAVIOR

To repeat the basic premise, our behavior is *shaped* by the result it produces. Our behavior is *selected* by the result we *expect* it to produce. An individual who perceives the result as sufficiently favorable will react accordingly, and the behavior will happen.

Although behavior is a complex thing, the key to motivating others lies in determining the results they would find favorable or positive. There are certain universal results we all want out of life, but it is essential that we learn to analyze individuals to determine the specific results *they* seek.

Recognize that different people may behave in a similar way for entirely different reasons; that is, they expect different results. For example, I may read a certain book because I feel it will broaden my knowledge, help me advance in my work, and make it possible for me to earn more money (my motive). You may read the same book in order to become more conversant among your colleagues and make you look more important (ego). Still a third person may read the same book to gain a sense of achievement. A fourth person may find reading relaxing, regardless of the book's contents. Still another may be practicing for greater reading speed and comprehension. Each of us may have a totally different reason (motive) for behaving in the same way. In each case, however, had there been no perceived positive result, none of us would have read the book. Again, behavior is selected because of the result we expect it to produce.

To illustrate further, here are some common behaviors and some possible perceived results which may prompt the behaviors:

BEHAVIOR ("If I . . .)	RESULT (. . . it will . . .")
Eat	Stop my hunger
Work hard	Salvage my employment
Save money	Make a vacation trip possible
Earn more	Give me a higher standard of living
Get an education	Make life easier and more enjoyable
Join a country club	Give me more prestige
Buy life insurance	Protect my family from destitution
Buy a Cadillac	Make me look more successful
Drink alcohol	Make me feel relaxed and help me forget my worries
Grow a beard	Make me look more sophisticated
Grow a moustache	Make me look more adult
Buy elevator shoes	Make me look taller and more important
Succeed in my job	Give me more prestige and sense of accomplishment
Open my own business	Give me more independence
Write my own book	Provide more income and sense of pride

BEHAVIOR ("If I . . .")	RESULT (. . . it will . . .")
Swat a fly	Help me avoid aggravation
Take an annual physical	Help me avoid illness and loss of income
Display a trophy	Show proof of superior ability
Jog	Improve my health and help me live longer
Chew out a subordinate	Make me feel superior
Display good manners	Make me socially acceptable
Win an argument	Make me look intelligent and superior

Everything we do, we do for a reason, that is, a positive result we expect our behavior to produce, or to avoid a negative result we don't want to experience. Literally, you have lived your entire life in a constant search of positive results and in the avoidance of negative results. The "Law of Effect" has been with you since the day you were born and will be with you until the day you die. People do things because of what happens to them when they do it. Likewise, people avoid doing things because of what might happen to them (negative results) if they do it.

DETERMINING TARGET RESULTS

Again, the key to motivating another person lies in the ability to determine the results *he* perceives as worthwhile. Don't make the mistake of assuming what results *you* find most favorable will be the same for others. Every one of us has his or her own set of results he or she pursues.

Another leading behaviorist, the late Dr. Abraham Maslow of Brandeis University, developed a theory which makes it possible for us to categorize the results people seek into five basic groups.* Although Dr. Maslow used the term *needs*, rather than *results*, they are essentially the same. Maslow

* Abraham H. Maslow, *Motivation and Personality.* New York: Harper & Row, 1954.

found that all of us seek five basic sets of results which shape our behavior:

1. Results which enhance our physical well-being—food, shelter, comfort, sex, exercise, rest, and so on.
2. Results which strengthen our sense of security—physical security, financial security, freedom from harm, freedom from worry or fear.
3. Results which increase our social acceptance by others—to be an accepted individual, to be an important part of the human race, to belong, to identify with others, to have our circle of friends and colleagues.
4. Results which enhance our ego—a favorable self-image, self-respect, esteem, recognition, a feeling of importance, a sense of independence, control of situations, freedom to make decisions and to control our own destiny.
5. Results which provide a sense of achievement—to reach our full potential, to be the best, to win, to accomplish, to excel over others, to gain a sense of fulfillment and satisfaction, and to develop a feeling of appreciation and love.

Although they may use different terms, most leading behaviorists seem to agree with the findings of Dr. Maslow. Basically, we are all seeking the same *kinds* of things in life, even though our specific motives are different. We spend our entire lives in constant pursuit of the results we find rewarding or favorable and in avoiding the results we find unrewarding or unfavorable.

To illustrate behaviors which may produce various results, consider the following:

Results which enhance our physical well-being:
Take an annual physical examination
Eat properly
Ride a bicycle
Give up smoking

Play tennis
Plant a garden
Buy an air conditioner
Buy a new mattress

Results which strengthen our sense of security:
Open a savings account
Buy insurance
Install a burglar alarm or smoke detector
Expand our education
Work harder on the job
Invest in a retirement plan
Take a course in karate
Get a college education

Results which increase our social acceptance by others:
Display proper courtesy and manners
Join a bowling league
Attenda company picnic
Participate in a civic organization
Maintain good personal hygiene
Dress properly
Become conversant in popular subjects
Entertain friends and colleagues

Results which enhance our ego:
Achieve more to gain recognition
Improve our knowledge and skills
Buy expensive clothing, automobiles, jewelry, and the like
Display plaques and trophies
Boast about achievements
Participate in competitive activities
Practice one-upmanship
Display diplomas, certificates, and so forth
Join a country club
Buy elevator shoes
Grow a beard or moustache

Drop names
Live in an expensive neighborhood
Live beyond our incomes

Results which provide a sense of achievement:
Build model airplanes, boats, and the like
Write and publish a book
Become the best in our profession
Run for a political office
Complete an advanced degree
Engage in competitive activities
Build a business of our own
Demand perfection in our own work
Educate our children
Win a contest
Set and achieve personal goals in life
Learn to fly an airplane
Learn a foreign language

Obviously, there is a great amount of overlap, but then, different people do the same thing for different reasons. You may run for a public office for the sheer thrill of winning, just to prove to yourself you can do it. I may run for office because of the publicity and recognition it would provide (ego). Another may seek office in order to implement a specific political program. Still another may seek the higher income it would provide. Our behavior is determined by the results *we* expect it to produce for *us*. The expected result becomes the motive that triggers the behavior.

Effect on Buying Habits

Look back through the lists of behaviors for a moment and notice how they affect our buying habits. Think of the countless purchases we make because of the results they give us. We buy things to enhance our ego. We buy things to promote physical well-being. We buy things to gain social acceptance and financial security. Our purchases are constantly determined by our motives. Nearly every behavior previously listed involves a purchase, either directly or indirectly. I hope you are beginning to understand why a basic knowledge of motivational fundamentals is essential to the process of selling. They are inseparable.

It is not our objective here to develop an in-depth study of the subject of motivation, but rather to lay some basic groundwork as it relates to selling. Further study, however, would be of enormous help to any salesperson. Libraries are well stocked with the writings of B.F. Skinner, Frederick Herzberg, Abraham Maslow, Douglas McGregor, and many others who have contributed to our understanding of motivation. Further studies are available from practitioners who have validated and applied the behaviorists' contributions in the business world over the years.* These writings provide real-life experiences in the application of motivational techniques.

Purchasing habits can be directly related to the findings of both Thorndike and Maslow. Every purchase you or I make is triggered by the result we expect it to produce. We buy things which help provide physical well-being, including food, clothing, medicines, air conditioners, and exercise equipment. We buy things which give us a sense of security: insurance plans, smoke detectors, handguns, fire extinguishers, investment programs, and dead bolts for our doors. Even advanced education courses help ensure against joblessness. Think of the countless purchases we make to gain greater social acceptance: expensive clothing, houses, recreational programs, jewelry, group tours, and the like. It would be next to impossible to develop a complete list of purchases we make that appeal to our egos: expensive cars, boats, country club memberships, diamond rings, oil paintings, antique furniture, and many other items.

* J.F. Evered, *Shirt-Sleeves Management*, AMACOM, 1981. See also G.J. Lumsden, *Motivation in Management*, Chrysler Institute, 1974.

Emotional or Logical Buying?

Far more purchases are made on the basis of emotion than of pure logic. Think of the last several gifts you bought for your spouse or sweetheart. Just how logical were they? You will probably find that most were bought on an emotional basis. Now, getting someone to admit to emotional purchases is something else, but emotional buying is a way of life, especially for the American buyer. Just how logical is a mink coat? How many women wear a mink coat for the sole purpose of keeping warm? Just how logical is perfume, a diamond-studded wristwatch, a vacation in the Bahamas, a foreign sports car, a fifty-dollar bottle of champagne, or an antique brass bed? Emotion plays a big part in our buying habits.

Study television commercials for a few evenings and see how the advertising experts appeal to your emotions. They know how to strum your heartstrings until you reach for your checkbook. They know that emotional appeals are more successful than practical ones most often.

Does all this mean that our purchases are made solely on the basis of emotion? Of course not. Logic will dictate that you need to wear a wristwatch to keep from missing appointments. However, in all probability emotion will dictate *which* one you buy. From a logical standpoint, we need an automobile for transportation, but emotion will play a major role in the selection of it.

Reason or logic comes into play when we consider such things as price, quality, profit, durability, guarantee, investments for resale, health care items, and basic necessities. One certainly doesn't get very emotional when purchasing a loaf of bread, prescription drugs, corporate stocks, a car muffler, or a shovel. Little emotion is involved as a purchasing agent buys materials, furniture, fixtures, and equipment for an employer. Business purchases are usually made on the basis of logic, but personal purchases are something else. Here, emotion plays a big role, and sales appeals are made toward fear, pride, gain, imitation, shame, assurance, pity, loyalty, love, sex, enjoyment, and happiness.

The successful salesperson will appeal to both logic and emotion whenever possible. Either appeal, however, must be aimed toward some kind of result that the customer perceives as rewarding, positive, or favorable. From a motivational standpoint, we must learn ways of uncovering those results that the customer would find favorable. These are the customer's motivational triggers. Once we determine the results the customer perceives as favorable, we are in a position to make a sales presentation that is more likely to produce the behavior we want—the signing of the order.

3

Determining Target Results

To review the basic concept presented in Chapter 2, our behavior is determined by the result we expect it to produce. In other words, people do things because of what happens to them when they do it. Behavior is a means to a result.

If we understand this concept, we are ready to apply it in a selling situation. The behavior we want from the customer is the signing of the order. Therefore, we must determine what result would seem favorable to the customer if the order is signed. If the customer perceives the result, or outcome, to be sufficiently valuable, the behavior will occur.

LEARNING TO READ THE CUSTOMER

To be effective in motivating employees, a supervisor must learn how to "read" employees and determine the results each seeks out of life. This identifies the employee's motivational triggers so the supervisor knows which motivational efforts are most likely to succeed. The ability to read other people is an extremely powerful tool to any manager or salesperson.*

* J.F. Evered, *Shirt-Sleeves Management,* AMACOM, 1981.

People surround themselves with signals that tell the world what turns them on. Among those signals are what they wear, what they drive, what they hang on their walls, what they place on shelves, what they talk about, and so forth. We are constantly transmitting our motivational triggers to others. As does a supervisor, a salesperson must learn to read these signals because they provide a definite advantage in the selling situation. Sales presentations can emphasize those things (results) that the customer seeks. For example, if we knew, through the signals, that a customer was projecting a strong image of success and wanted to be perceived as a successful person, we would be in a position to emphasize the elements of success that our product or service might help him achieve. Conversely, the overly cautious or conservative customer may be more concerned with security. Perhaps our product would present less gamble, protect his position, and strengthen his financial security. These appeals would be much more meaningful as to the results he would expect. The appeals would be on target.

In a selling situation, however, you may have little time to size up a customer. You may have to make a quick judgment as to the kind of person he is. Take a quick look around for signals. What's on his walls, his desk, his bookshelves? What kind of image is he projecting? How does he speak? What does he talk about? Does he seem to be insecure, confident, domineering, hungry for social contact? Does he seem achievement-oriented, the picture of success? A cursory observation may provide clues to the type of sales presentation that would be most successful. I suggest you review the five sets of results that shape behavior, listed in Chapter 2 on "Fundamentals of Motivation." You should attempt to identify which category best fits your customer, if possible.

Obviously, the more you know about your customer, the greater your advantage in appealing to his or her specific motivational triggers. Over a period of time you will learn more and more about each customer, and tailor-made presentations will become a way of life for you. A later chapter is devoted to developing a better understanding of your customer.

Tipping the Sales Scale

Reading your customers' signals will help you determine the results each one seeks, but you will need more specific, in-depth information to keep your selling on target. Don't make the mistake of assuming that *your* motivational triggers will be important to others. That assumption has lost many a sale. You must determine what is important to the customer. You must determine what is in the customer's mind, because it is there that a buying decision will be made. Your objective is to give the right information so the customer can make a wise decision. It is *his* thinking that we must influence if we are to make the sale. We must help him see that the expected result of buying is of sufficient value to him. This value perception in the customer's mind is conceptualized in Figure 3, the "Sales Scale."

Basically, the customer is weighing two things in his mind—what he'll have to pay for an item versus what he's

Figure 3. The "sales scale."

going to get out of it (result). He is simply asking himself, "Is it worth it?"

If, in the customer's mind, price outweighs value, there is no way you can close the sale. It isn't worth it to him. If, in his mind, price and value are equal, you *might* get the sale. At least he feels it would be a fair exchange. If, however, value outweighs price in his mind, that's when you close the sale. It is now worth more to him than the price you're asking.

Please note the four key words *in the customer's mind*. This is extremely important, because value is not in the product; it's in the customer's mind. Value is nothing more than a measure of how badly we want something. It's a mental situation. That's why we, as salespersons, are able to influence it.

Our job in selling is to get the value side of the scale to outweigh the price side. This brings us to one of the great tragedies in the field of selling. The vast majority of people in selling are earning less than their potential because they're going at it in the wrong way, the difficult and unproductive way. How?

If we were to divide this sales scale down the middle, we would find that the left-hand side of the scale represents one kind of language, and the right-hand side represents a completely different language—and the majority of people in selling are speaking the *wrong* language. What's the difference between them?

The left-hand language is a *manufacturing* language. It tells us how the product is made, how it's put together, what it is made of, and so forth. Actually, this is where a price comes from. It is the accumulation of profit margins, cost of labor, materials, handling, shipping, and warehousing that establishes a price.

The right-hand language on the scale is a *selling* language, the language so few salesmen have learned to speak. It is the easier and more productive language to speak. It is the only language that makes sense to the customer.

In other words, the left side tells us *how* the product was made, whereas the right side tells us *why* it was made that way, that is, what it's going to do for the customer. It tells us what results the customer can expect from the product.

Since value is in the customer's mind, it's obvious that's the only thing you can influence. That's why we say in selling, "You can't change the price, but you can change the value of the merchandise." Oh, sure, we may be able to dicker a little with price, but there's a definite limit as to how much. But there's no limit as to how much value we can add, and adding value to the scale is what selling is all about.

If we are to add value to the right side of the scale, it is obvious that we must determine those things of greatest value to the customer, that is, the *results* the customer would perceive of greatest value if he or she buys.

If your cursory observation of the customer has not provided any clues to help you, your next step is to dig out as much information as possible. This can be accomplished through careful questioning.

Ask and Listen

Few people in selling have ever mastered the art of questioning. Usually they think that talking is more important than listening. But using questions is the only way you can find out exactly what is on the customer's mind. Through questions you determine an individual's likes, dislikes, and attitudes, and learn the specific results that would be most valuable to him or her. It is absolutely essential that you learn these things if your selling is to be on target. Remember, as long as you are talking you aren't learning a thing. And when you ask a question, for goodness sake, *listen* to the customer's reply. Listening with comprehension has always been one of the most difficult disciplines to teach salespeople. The salesperson who asks a question usually will ignore the customer's reply. He is too busy thinking up his next statement, designed to astound. Don't think that customer can't tell when you are not listening to him.

Through questions you can gain valuable information that will help you make a meaningful sales presentation. Questions can be used to verify information. Questions will keep the customer's attention focused where you want it. The liberal use of questions will balance the conversation between you and the customer, an extremely valuable sales technique. Although in keeping with popular practice I have been using the term *sales presentation*, I really don't like it. The term *presentation* connotes one-way communication; that is, something, if not everything, is being *presented* to the customer. I much prefer to use the term *sales interview*, which is a two-way communication. That's the way it should be. Among the top salespeople I have met, I find that most of them talk about 40 percent of the time and listen about 60 percent. Questions gain customer involvement, and top salespeople know how important that is.

Open-ended Questions

Open-ended questions are those that cannot be answered with a simple yes or no. They are perhaps the most valuable kind of questions when you are gathering vital information. They are often referred to as fact-finding questions. They invite customers to talk, to express their feelings, attitudes, likes, dislikes, and doubts. An enormous amount of information can be gained through questioning.

The best open-ended questions are those beginning with *why, how, what, when, where,* and *who*. Naturally, the specific questions you would use would be determined by the product or service you sell, but let's list a few to illustrate how they probe for important information you will need during the sales interview:

"Mr. McKay, what steps have you taken in the past to increase your inventory turnover?"

"Mrs. Sellers, how would you feel about increasing your speed in handling monthly billings by 25 percent?"

"Mr. Allen, what effect would it have on your business if you reduced your service costs by 15 percent?"

"What are the primary services you expect from a supplier, Mrs. Evans?"

"What advertising assistance would be most helpful to you, Ms. Walters?"

"When do you find it most convenient for suppliers to call on you, Mrs. Jackson?"

"Why are you concerned about fast delivery, Mr. Beck?"

"In the past, Mr. Yates, who seemed to serve your specific needs best?"

"How have you been able to solve your warehousing problems in the past, Mr. Garrett?"

"What specific problems would you anticipate in changing suppliers, Mr. Wilson?"

"What type of features do you look for in a house, Mrs. Bellamy?"

"How would this plan fit into your financial future, Ms. Martin?"

As you can see, these questions invite the customer to expose attitudes, feelings, and information. They help you determine the specific results the customer expects from a product or service. Once you have determined what the customer expects, you are in a position to show the customer how your product or service will produce that result. Most often, if you carefully plan your questions, customers will tell you exactly what to sell them and how to sell it.

I can remember demonstrating this technique hundreds of times several years ago. I was the director of training for one of the major oil companies and was responsible for training service station dealers as well as company sales personnel. At that time, tubeless tires were relatively new on the market and most car owners were reluctant to accept the new innovation in tires. Many actually insisted on putting tubes in them anyway.

During the sales interview I would ask a question such as, "Mr. Gates, if you had unlimited finances and could afford to build the ideal automobile tire, what would you expect that tire to do for you?" Invariably, the reply would run in these veins: "Well, I would want it to get good mileage, be economical in cost, run smooth and quiet, resist blowouts, and give me a comfortable ride." Can you see how the customer was backing himself into a corner? My tire could offer him everything he wanted in a tire. He was actually eliminating every reason for not buying.

If I could only demonstrate, to the customer's satisfaction, how the tubeless feature protected him against blowouts, I would have a sale—and I could. I would take a toy balloon, blow it up, and puncture it with a pin. Bang! I would blow up two balloons, one inside the other, and explain how it represented a tire and a tube. Again, when I punctured it with a pin—bang! I would blow up one more balloon and attach a small piece of Scotch tape to the side of it, explaining how it was attached the way the butyl liner is attached inside a tubeless tire. When I punctured through the tape and balloon with a pin, nothing happened. The clinching question that usually closed the sale was, "Mr. Gates, which would you rather have, a blowout or a slow-out?"

We used the same questioning technique to sell the newly developed detergent motor oils when people were not yet ready to accept them. We would ask, "Sir, if you had millions of dollars available for research on the ideal motor oil, what would you expect that oil to do for you?" The customer would invariably tell us the very things the new detergent oil was designed to do, that is, protect the engine when it was either hot or cold, reduce friction, extend engine life, and keep the engine clean. When he was finished enumerating what he wanted, all we had to do was show him the specifications on the back of the can and say, "Here it is!" Customers will always tell you what results are important to them if you pose your questions carefully. Once you know what is important to the customer, you can sell intelligently and more effectively.

Questions serve another important function in selling; that is, they tend to minimize resistance when it comes time to close the sale. The reason is simple. Your selling effort has been on target because you used questions to identify the target, the specific results the customer expected from the product or service. The effective use of questions is the only way you can identify the specific targets. Otherwise, you will be shotgunning with a solution, hoping you can find a customer with a matching problem. That is a time-consuming and ineffective way of selling, if you can call it selling.

You should develop a list of effective fact-finding questions and make them a part of your very life. Naturally, the questions must be pertinent to the product or service you are selling. A little imagination will help you develop some appropriate questions. Just ask yourself this question as you develop the list: "If I could know anything I wanted to know about this customer that would give me an advantage in the selling situation, what would I want to know?" Then develop a list of questions that will uncover the things you need to know.

As you pose questions, use the customer's name as frequently as is comfortable. It has often been said that a person's name is the most important word in his vocabulary. There is no more beautiful music to a person's ear than his name spoken.

Closed-end Questions

Most closed-end questions can be answered with a simple yes or no and are used to confirm or to gain specific information. Most of these questions will begin with *do, did, don't, won't, is, isn't, are,* and so forth. Here are some examples:

"Do you have . . . ?"
"Didn't you say that . . . ?"
"Do you currently use . . . ?"
"Don't you agree that . . . ?"
"Isn't this what you want?"
"Are you now . . . ?"
"Are we in agreement that . . . ?"
"Are you presently . . . ?"

These questions are used to confirm information and to fix certain key points in the customer's mind. Other closed-end questions may be used to gain specific information and do not require elaboration from the customer. For example:

"What is your inventory closing date?"
"When do you normally need . . . ?"
"Who is your head buyer?"
"How many do you normally stock?"
"Who is your present supplier?"

Effective selling usually consists of a balance of open-ended and closed-end questions, both used liberally. But remember, questions are of little value if you don't listen carefully to the customer's replies. The information the customer gives you identifies your selling targets.

Reflective Questions

Reflective questions not only invite the customer to keep talking but are also used to clarify information to be certain you understand correctly. Some of the reflective questions that invite the customer to keep talking or to elaborate on a point might include:

"Oh?"
"How's that?"
"In what way?"
"Is that right?"
"How do you mean?"
"For example?"

A reflective question puts the ball back into the customer's court and invites him or her to keep talking on a certain point. A lot of vital information can be gained, information that helps you determine your sales targets.

Other reflective questions can be used to clarify information, for example, "Then you feel that . . . ?", "Then you have found that . . . ?", "Then you agree that . . . ?", "Then you need . . . ?", or "You emphasized that . . . ?" The customer will not only answer the question but will usually elaborate the point even further, giving you still more vital information.

RESULTS ARE INDIVIDUALIZED

People buy a product because of what it will do for them, nothing more. If they believe that the result it will produce for them is sufficiently valuable, they will buy. Our job in selling is to get them to see the full value of the results our product will provide. If you are to succeed in selling, it is absolutely essential that you keep this concept foremost in your mind. People buy things for *their* reasons, not *yours*.

Don't sell a mattress; sell a night's sleep, freedom from backache, less tossing and turning, a more energetic tomorrow. Don't sell motor oil; sell engine protection, longer engine life, fewer engine repairs, a better investment, peace of mind. Don't sell an insurance policy; sell protection, freedom from worry, a college education for the children, guaranteed savings, and so forth. It isn't the product the customer wants; it's the result the product or service produces. Results justify a purchase in the customer's mind. Concentrate on the results.

A paint salesman wouldn't get very far stressing pigment, binders, oxidation inhibitors, and viscosity. Those are meaningless to a customer. What the customer wants is results, that is, long-lasting protection, ease of application, easy cleanup, no fading, and an appearance to be proud of.

To repeat, our behavior is selected by the results we expect it to produce. Therefore, a salesperson must help the customer see the results he could expect if he buys the product. Just remember, the customer doesn't buy the product; he buys the result the product will produce for him. Effective selling *always* stresses the results the customer can expect from the product or service.

In no way does this mean we should ignore the features of the product. Those features play an important part in selling, but they only tell how the product is made, what goes into it, and so forth. They are the physical characteristics of the product that determine a price. But every single feature in a product is there to produce some kind of result for the customer. It is up to the salesperson to translate those features into meaningful results for the customer. Remember, the buying decision will be determined by how much value the customer places on the result.

Earlier I mentioned that one of the great tragedies in the field of selling is that most salespeople are speaking the wrong language, a manufacturing language that stresses features and leaves the translation of results up to the customer. Features justify a price; results justify a purchase. Feature selling adds very little value on the sales scale.

Salespeople tend to stress product features for two reasons. The first is their overfamiliarization with the product. They have spent a great deal of time learning everything possible about the product. As a result they feel comfortable talking about it. They are impressed with the product and think customers will be equally impressed. Unfortunately, the customer doesn't share this excitement about the product and is concerned only with what the product will do for him. As the great master salesman, Bill Gove, once put it, "The customer doesn't care how good we make our goods, only how good our goods make him."

The biggest single reason salespeople don't use results-oriented selling is based on two assumptions they make, one of which is correct, and the other, incorrect.

Assumption number one is, "The customer knows all those benefits and I'd sound silly if I mentioned them." On most products this assumption may be true. The customer does know many of the results he would receive.

Assumption number two is that the customer will be *thinking* of the results. That assumption is incorrect. The results are buried in the customer's memory bank and he has never been disciplined to dig them out. Unless the customer is made to think about the results and made aware of them at the moment, they're not even on the scale. They weigh nothing as far as your sale is concerned. It's the salesman's job to *put* them on the scale by talking about them and making the customer aware of them. The customer will voluntarily put very little value on the scale. That's the salesman's job.

Until the result side of the scale outweighs the price side, you aren't going to close the sale. Why let the customer dribble the value on the scale with a teaspoon? The salesman can put the value up there with a large scoop because he knows how important and necessary it is.

Selling would be easy if we could use Gestapo techniques. If we could tell a customer, for instance, "This charcoal grill is made of cast aluminum, which won't rust. Now you (mister customer) sit down here and write a list of fifteen reasons it would be better for you." That would force the customer through the mental gymnastics of thinking up all the reasons he would be better off with the cast aluminum charcoal grill.

American buyers, including purchasing agents, have never been disciplined to do that, and they aren't going to do it. If you subscribe to the philosophy of the sales scale, that is, that you must present enough value to offset the total price the customer must pay, then you understand that the only results on the value side of the scale are those the customer is consciously thinking of at the moment. If the customer isn't thinking of them, they're not on the scale.

The results you so adroitly place on the scale won't stay there long. They slide off and hit the floor, because you or the customer changes subjects, or either of you is distracted by a question, or an objection is raised. That's why it is so important to use a *summary* just before closing a sale. It is during the summary that you pick up all the major points (results), put them back on the scale (in the customer's mind), get him thinking about them again, and go for the close while they are still on the scale.

The kind of results the customer will expect the product to create will depend on the individual customer. The retail customer, or the end user of the product, would expect a set of results different from those expected by a wholesaler or dealer who will be reselling the product at a profit. The retail customer's buying decision is far more likely to be made on the basis of emotion, whereas the dealer will view it in a more logical way. The dealer, however, also expects the product to create some specific results. He is interested in a product with high turnover, profits, satisfied customers, fewer service problems, and ease of selling. The consumer, on the other hand, is looking for such results as convenience, ease of use, comfort, durability, safety, savings, and pride of ownership.

As a brief review, the behavior we want from the customer is the signing of the order—the purchase. If the behavior is determined by the results it is expected to produce, then it becomes obvious that all selling effort must be aimed toward helping the customer perceive maximum value or results. We must stress the positive results the customer will receive and the negative results he will avoid if he buys. Therefore, results become the prime target in selling, as illustrated in Figure 4.

In a sense, the avoidance of a negative result is a positive to the customer. Avoiding the things we don't want to happen to us is the motive for many of our purchases. For example, we buy life insurance to protect our families from destitution in the event of our death. Perhaps it protects our children from the necessity of dropping out of college. We purchase smoke detectors to help us avoid disastrous losses in the event of a fire. The negative is the potential loss; the positive is the peace of mind.

Manufacturers buy high-quality (often more expensive) raw materials to avoid the problem of dissatisfied customers and

Figure 4. Results—the prime target.

high service costs, results they don't want to experience. Millions of airline passengers purchase various tablets to help them avoid the discomfort and embarrassment of air sickness. Insecticides are purchased to avoid lawn damage. We buy homeowner's insurance to avoid being financially wiped out in the event of a fire. We pay for regular physical examinations to avoid or prevent serious illness and its financial burden. The list of products and services we buy for the purpose of avoiding losses is endless. But, keep in mind, these products and services have some positive results as well.

Through observation and questioning, the salesperson is able to determine the positive results the customer wants and the negative results the customer wishes to avoid. Once these are determined, all selling effort can remain on target. The salesperson who selects target results on the basis of guesswork, intuition, or assumptions is in serious trouble and his or her sales results will be determined by sheer luck. Selling, in a sense, is like playing the piano. If you want to play the piano for your own amusement, you can afford to play by ear. But if you plan to earn your living at it, you had better learn to play by note. This book is designed to teach you how to read the music.

The salesman who assumes he knows what results the customer expects will invariably make a *presentation,* a one-way communication. The salesman who is genuinely interested in learning what is most important to the customer will conduct a sales *interview,* a two-way communication. The latter will more often result in a sale. Therefore, from this point forward, I will use the terms *sales interview* and *sales situation.*

FACETS OF LOGIC AND EMOTION

Regardless of what you are selling, you are always appealing both to a person's logic and to his or her emotions, two entirely different personalities in one customer. On the side of logic, you are appealing to a desire for profit, gain, economic security, perceived needs for materials, tools, and equipment, and return on investment. On the emotional side, you help the customer obtain results that satisfy psychological needs, enhance self-image, give a sense of security, relieve worry, help gain social acceptance, heighten sense of pride, increase importance in the eyes of others, and give a sense of independence, of control, and of achievement.

Neiman-Marcus is probably the best example of appealing to both logic and emotion. Stanley Marcus built a financial retail empire on the concept of making maximum appeal to all the senses. In his uncompromising search for the very best in merchandise and service, this dual set of human needs served as his guide. Furthermore, his buyers never lost sight of the needs of middle- and lower-income customers as they continued to select quality merchandise. Contrary to the belief of many, Neiman-Marcus does not limit its merchandise to the exotic, the unbelievably expensive, or the one-of-a-kind. Those items are ever present, but Neiman-Marcus has merchandise to appeal to any income level, competitive with any major department store. The principal difference lies in quality, an area in which Stanley Marcus was uncompromising. He understood both the financial needs and emotional needs of his customers.*

Salespeople often overlook these important psychological needs of a customer and concentrate on the pure logic of the purchase. Consequently, the product has only half the potential appeal to the customer. Many a sale has been lost, not because a product wouldn't do the job, not because it didn't carry the lowest price, quickest delivery, and the best terms, but because of failure to produce the psychological results the customer needs. The results could have been there had the salesperson recognized the psychological or emotional side of the customer.

You may be asking yourself, "Just how emotional is a corporate purchasing agent, or a dealer, or a wholesaler, or a physi-

* Stanley Marcus, *Quest for the Best*. New York: The Viking Press, 1979.

cian?" Don't kid yourself. Those people have just as many psychological needs as you or I. That purchasing agent wants to look good in the eyes of his management. A wise decision could very well enhance his career advancement. It could be a significant psychological blow to him if he makes a poor decision. He takes a great amount of pride in saving corporate funds. It enhances his self-image to report his successes to management. He feels a sense of achievement in maintaining a proper balance of turnover in raw materials. Wise decisions heighten his sense of security. Emotional needs? You bet! Every last one of us takes pride in making wise decisions.

A physician takes pride in seeing his patients recover quickly as a result of his decisions in prescribing medication. His self-image is enhanced when he makes wise decisions. He is proud that he is up to date on the latest pharmaceuticals and is able to prescribe properly. He is secure in the knowledge that his professional ability makes him less vulnerable to malpractice accusations. Use of the latest and best surgical instruments and diagnostic equipment gives him a great sense of satisfaction and achievement. The salesman who recognizes and appeals to these psychological needs, as well as to the economic needs of the physician, is far more likely to succeed than the salesman who discusses only the product, packaging, price, delivery, and terms.

A housewife may be far less interested to know that waterless cookware will preserve the vitamin content of foods than that her husband will appreciate her cooking more. Her psychological needs may outweigh logic when she makes her buying decision.

A farmer is concerned about increasing his crop yield by applying agricultural fertilizer, but don't think he doesn't take pride in having the most lush crop in the area—a crop that is taller, greener, and healthier. It gives him a great sense of achievement to have the highest yield and best quality among his neighbors.

Personally, I feel a great sense of pride and satisfaction in the complete insurance program I have established to protect my family and myself. I am proud of the decisions I have made, with the help of a good salesman, in establishing a sound financial program. I feel that I have achieved something important. Emotion and psychological needs played a big part in it.

Appliance dealers and equipment dealers take pride in having fewer service calls, in receiving fewer customer complaints, and in developing a reputation for reliability and quality among their customers.

As customers, each of us has a logical side as well as an emotional or psychological side. The salesperson who recognizes this and appeals to both is the one who gets the business. Maximum sales will always come to the salesperson who appeals to both logic and emotion in *every* sales interview with *every* customer. Not to do so will reduce sales effectiveness by 50 percent and will reduce the salesperson's income by an equal amount. As you plan a sales interview, always ask two key questions: "What logical results will my product create for the customer? What emotional results will it produce?" A sales interview that answers both will help you succeed where others have failed.

I recall a salesman three years ago who did a good job of appealing to my emotions as well as to my logic (although it turned out later that the salesman's reliability was somewhat questionable). Now that both of our children were through college, working, and successful, my wife and I had decided that our home in Dallas, Texas, would be permanent through retirement. We therefore decided to make a few additions to the home so that we could enjoy it more. The largest addition was the installation of a swimming pool.

The salesman's appeal to our logic was minimal. He stated that the pool would be a great source of exercise and that the addition of a pool would enhance our property value in the event we should ever sell. I might say, parenthetically, he failed to mention what it would do to our property taxes.

But from the psychological side, he really poured it on. He talked at great length about pride of ownership, how we would enjoy having friends and neighbors over to swim. He described elaborate poolside parties. He talked about the suntans we could display. He even designed a beautiful pool shape, somewhat the shape of a peanut, which would be something not every pool owner has. I believe he described it as something above and beyond the ordinary. He designed terraced rock planters around it to give, as he called it, that "expensive sunken effect."

We are, of course, extremely proud of the pool, but if I look at the situation objectively, I must admit there is a lot more psychological than logical justification for building a swimming pool. That is probably true for most people who build a pool, but they rarely admit it.They probably try to rationalize it with a lot of logic. The point is, that salesman knew it was more important to appeal to my emotions than to my logic. He was a good salesman. Unfortunately, he didn't think that following up after the sale was important. He had his commission and didn't want any more to do with it.

Again, as you plan any sales call, plan it around both logical and psychological appeals. You are always selling to two customers, namely, the logical side and the emotional side of your customer. Appealing to both will greatly enhance your chance of closing the sale. Give every customer both barrels.

4

The Source
of
Solutions

There is nothing in selling that can't be summed up in two sentences: "You have a problem. I have the best solution." The purpose of selling is to solve the customer's problems, whether they are logical or psychological, real or imagined, personal or professional. A salesperson is a problem solver. The customer looks to the salesperson for a solution to the problems. What the customer wants is results, results that solve problems.

As discussed earlier, the salesperson uncovers the problems through observation and questioning, and then determines how the product or service will solve them. The solution to problems lies in the features built into the product. Nothing is designed into a product that isn't intended to do something for a customer, to produce a desired result, or to help the customer avoid an undesirable result. Therefore, it is essential for sales personnel to know as much as possible about their products. They must translate those features into something meaningful to the customers, that is, the *results* the customer can expect the product to produce.

The amount of product knowledge salespeople must have

covers the entire spectrum, from basic familiarization to a complete and exhaustive knowledge. Some salespersons deal with a single product, others with several thousand. The technical nature of a product, too, will dictate the detailed knowledge a salesperson must have. For example, a salesman who sells office copying machines may also be required to service the copier. In that case, an exhaustive and detailed knowledge would be essential.

Men and women who sell pharmaceuticals must have an extensive knowledge of chemistry and physiology in order to discuss results, side effects, care, storage, dosage, and the accompanying precautions.

But a detailed and exhaustive knowledge of a product doesn't necessarily make a good salesperson. If that weren't true, an auto mechanic would be the best car salesman, and a laboratory research chemist would be the best saleswoman for plastics, resins, petrochemicals, and pharmaceuticals.

It is impossible for certain salespersons ever to gain a detailed and exhaustive knowledge of their products because of the sheer volume of products they sell. Some deal in hundreds or thousands of products and must repeatedly turn to specification catalogs for specific information. But the ability to *find* accurate information immediately is the hallmark of successful salespeople. They have a detailed and exhaustive knowledge of reference manuals. This is true of those who sell raw materials to manufacturers; those who sell replacement parts, broad-spectrum chemicals, or accessories; and many others with a broad line of products.

The fact remains, however, the more you know about the various features of your product, the more you are able to show customers how it will produce results for them—and results are the only thing they are interested in. It is impossible for a salesperson to know too much about a product, as long as he or she presents it in terms of what it will do for the customer. If you don't know your product's features, you will have a difficult time convincing your customer that it will produce the desired results. At least you will have a difficult time validating your claims. Again, the source of the desired results lies in the features built into the product. It is your job to translate those features into the only thing that interests a customer—results.

LEARNING ABOUT THE PRODUCT

The sources to which you can turn to learn about the many features of your product are almost limitless. If you are with a company that has a formal sales training program, consider yourself lucky. During your training you will receive a lot of information about your product, as well as a lot of selling skills training. Grab every morsel of product information you can get. Read product manuals, product container labels, specification books, and any literature covering the subject. Read everything, but always in the context of "What results will this give my customer?"

If you ever have the opportunity, take a tour of the manufacturing plant where the product is made. This is a regular part of most formalized sales training programs. During my years as training director for a major oil company, our regular sales training program included special tours of a refinery, a battery manufacturing company, a passenger tire plant, a grease manufacturing plant, and a plant that manufactured automotive fan belts, heater hoses, and radiator hoses. The information we gained was invaluable, but was always studied from the standpoint of "what will it do for the customer?" That's the information we had to have if we were to succeed in selling the products, whether to distributors, retailers, or consumers. We had to know how the product was made if we were to understand what results it would produce for the customer. Furthermore, the tours through the various manufacturing plants gave us a great amount of confidence in the product we would sell.

If you do not have a formal sales training program, you may be left, to a degree, to your own devices to learn about your product. If possible, take the product apart, see how it is made or put together, see what materials are used. But always approach it from this standpoint, "Why is it made this way?" Then you are in a position to ask yourself, "What will this do for my customer?"

Ask your supplying company or employer for product information sheets. Study them religiously. Ask for a tour of the manufacturing plant. Ask for photographs. Talk to others who sell the same product, including wholesalers and retailers. If necessary, find out from your competitors. Pose as a potential customer and see how much information you can glean from them. I have often approached competitors, incognito, of course, under the guise that I was thinking about becoming their dealer in another area. Their salesmen were delighted to tell me anything I wanted to know about their products. Not only would they tell me all about their products and how they were made, but they gave me a host of selling ideas. Once in a rare while, one of them would even tell me what the product would do for me—a result.

As time goes on, products change. New innovations will be introduced, new uses will be found, and modifications will be made. There will be a never-ending change to the product you sell. Learn each change as it comes along, but learn it well in terms of the results it will produce for your customer. New products will be introduced. Learn every single thing you can about them. You will face changes in models, colors, sizes, designs, and features. As a sales representative, you are charged with the responsibility of knowing more about that product than anyone else, but always in terms of what result it will produce for the customer. Approach everything you do from this standpoint. Remember, you are a problem solver and a result producer. If your product won't produce results for your customer, get out of the territory or drop the product. Find a new one.

If you are dealing with an intangible product or service, it is equally essential that you understand every feature of it. It may be a little more difficult, however, digging out the features. It is necessary that you understand what is included and not included. Consider an insurance program, for example. You must know what is included in the coverage, what is excluded from coverage, and how it compares with competitive programs. Again, it is always necessary to learn your program from the standpoint, "What results will it produce for the customer?" This includes both logical and emotional results.

The information regarding features will include a comparison with other investments, the risks involved, and future opportunities to change, upgrade, or convert the program. A detailed study and interpretation of every clause in every single policy you sell is a must. Otherwise, you do not know what true services you are able to provide your customers. You must know what you can and cannot do when it comes to handling claims. A knowledgeable and conscientious insurance agent can be of enormous help in building a worry-free future for any individual, family, or business. The agent not only can help you get the positive results you want but can help you avoid the negative results you never want to experience. Therein lie the very purposes of any insurance program. Again, the customer isn't interested so much in what's being written into the policy, only what result the policy will produce for him in the event a claim becomes necessary.

TRANSLATING THE SOURCES INTO RESULTS

As we continue to develop a model that will help us keep the sales situation in a meaningful perspective, I will continue to review certain key points over and over again, even at the risk of your getting tired of them. I do not want you to lose this valuable perspective.

Review point number one: Behavior is shaped by the result it produces. The behavior we want is the signing of the order.

Review point number two: Our behavior is selected by the result we expect it to produce, that is, a positive result or the avoidance of a negative result.

Review point number three: The customer's buying decision will be determined by the value (result) he perceives as compared to the price he will have to pay, both financially and psychologically.

Review point number four: Our job in selling is to help the customer perceive maximum value in the product or service, that is, to get the right side of the sale (value) to outweigh the left side (price).

Review point number five: There is little we can do in selling to change the price, but there is no limit to how much we can add to the perceived value of the merchandise or service.

Earlier we discussed the important part product features play in selling. They are the source of results the customer can expect from a product. Our job in selling is to translate these important features into meaningful results (value) for the customer. If results are what the customer wants, results must become the primary target of our selling efforts. How, then, do we convert the product features into meaningful results?

There are two ways of going about it. You may wish to start with a feature of the product and tell the customer what results it will produce for him or her. Or you may wish to start with an important result and back it up with a feature.

Let's consider an example to illustrate the technique. Let's assume you are an appliance salesman in a large department store, conducting a sales interview with a woman who is considering a moderately priced gas range. Let's take just one of the many features of the range and convert it into meaningful results, using each of the techniques. First, let's begin with the feature, the source of results. "Mrs. Wilson, the door of this oven slips right off the hinges for ease of cleaning, which means no stooping and reaching to clean your oven. Cleaning up will be a lot faster and easier, so you can spend a lot less time in the kitchen and more time with your family." Now that wasn't difficult, was it? But did you notice the *bridge* we used between the feature and the result—"which means"?

Let's try it the other way, beginning with the result.

"Mrs. Wilson, with this oven, cleaning will be a lot quicker and easier with no stooping or reaching, because of this oven door that slips right off the hinges." Notice the *bridge* we used this time—"because of." The important thing is always to bridge the gap for the customer between result and feature (source of the result). Don't leave it to the customer's imagination. Bridging the gap is the salesman's job. Figure 5 shows this extended sales model with bridges between result and source.

Naturally, you can go either direction in bridging the gap. It is wise, however, to use both methods during a sales interview. This helps avoid monotony. Whichever method you use, the emphasis must always be on the expected results, the factor with the greatest influence on the buying decision and that adds the greatest value. The salesperson who overlooks this important point is in serious trouble.

Here is an idea I have always found effective in keeping my focus on the expected results. Whenever you mention one of your product's features, just imagine the customer replying, "So what?" Then you would force yourself to explain why the feature is there, what it will do for the customer, or the results the customer could expect from the feature. You would be speaking the right language, a selling language that builds value in the customer's mind to reach a favorable buying decision. From the customer's point of view, the most important question in all of selling is, "What's in it for me?" Your sales effort must be aimed toward answering that question.

That is the point at which we separate the clerks from the salespeople. A clerk's vocabulary seems to be limited to, "May

Figure 5. Bridges between result and source (product feature).

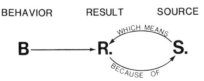

Figure 6. Result and source answer customer's questions.

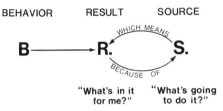

I help you?" and "Will that be cash or charge?" In no way can that be classified as selling. That person should not even be classified as a sales clerk. It's an insult to the selling profession. By no means do I imply that professional salespeople do not exist in retail stores. I have encountered many excellent salesmen and saleswomen in department stores, and so have you, but they are rare. Think how much improvement the clerk could make by adding just one word to his or her vocabulary, "*How* may I help you?"

Let's get back to converting the product features into meaningful results. The product features provide the source of the results, and remember to use the bridge as you make the translation for the customer.

As we see in Figure 6, *result* answers the customer's number one question, "What's in it for me?" The *source* (product feature) answers the customer's number two question, "What's going to do it?"

Result	Source
Won't roll off the desk	Hexagon shaped pencil
Easier to hold	
Less tiring	
No waiting to see	Instant-starting fluorescent light
Less chance of stubbing your toe	
Less aggravation	

Result	Source
No ink stains on clothing	Positive clip on fountain pen
Protects pen tip from damage	
No embarrassment	
Less dry cleaning	
Tip won't dry out	
Less cleaning of tip	
Less expensive	
Longer lasting	Furniture joints dadoed and glued
Better investment	
Stronger joints	
Greater surface area for glue	
Safer	
Greater trade-in value	
Safer tire	Tire with large road surface contact
Greater traction	
Longer lasting	
Better investment	
More comfort	
Avoids accidents	
Greater accuracy	Perfectly balanced rifle
More trophies	
More game	
More pride in hunting	
Less tiring to carry	
Greater resale value	
Less chance of slipping	Positive lock pliers
Fewer skinned knuckles	
Faster work	
Frees both hands	
Less work	Lightweight aluminum case on vacuum cleaner
Less tiring	
Finish work faster	

Result	Source
More time with family	
Less wear on carpet	
Fewer trips to store	Seven-day meat keeper compartment
Take advantage of food sales, less cost	
Offers variety	
Saves gasoline	
Allows once-a-week shopping	
Safe and nonpoisonous	Insect growth regulator mineral for cattle consumption
Balance of vitamins and minerals	
No harm to environment	
No withdrawal problems	
No mixing necessary, saves work	
Better digestion	
Writes distinct and fine line	5-mm nylon-bonded tip on ball-point pen
Greater precision	
Greater legibility	
Less chance of mistakes in reading	
Improved quality of handwriting	
More pride in work	
Greater reliability	
Easier to clean, less work	Textured steel door on freezer
Fingerprints will not show	
Less frequent cleaning	
Resists scratching and chipping	
More attractive	
Cleaner to handle	No-carbon paper
No carbon smears on hands	

Result	Source
Security of information	
No carbon disposal	
Greater legibility	
Automatically holds, de-frosts, cooks, or warms	Programmable microwave oven
Works while you are gone	
Food ready when you get home	
Saves time and work	
Avoid panic meal planning	
Last-minute meal decisions no problem	
Longer lasting	Asphalt roof shingles
Better investment	
Peace of mind	
Protection from neighboring fires	
Leakproof	
Fewer repair bills	
Neat appearance	Extra long shirttails
Fits taller people	
Less embarrassment	
Keeps condensation out	Double vapor barrier in the ceiling
Avoids stained ceilings, draperies, curtains, and carpeting	
Avoids repair bills	
Better investment	
Greater resale value	
You won't spend your nights scratching	Tent with mesh-covered door and windows
Cooler, better ventilation	
More comfortable	
Better visibility	
Lets light and breeze in, keeps bugs and snakes out	
More fun and enjoyment	

Some die-hard sales trainers will take issue with me on some of the items I listed under results and will say they are features or advantages. I won't argue with them because it is really immaterial.

The significant point is that the customer isn't interested in the feature of the product but only in the result he or she can expect from the feature. The listed examples show how value is built in the customer's mind. Look back over the examples and ask yourself, "What is it the customer really expects, features or results?" You and I both know the answer to this question. The customer is interested in what the feature or product is going to do for him, that is, the results the feature will produce. If you want to get results, talk results. If you fail to translate the features into meaningful results and leave the translation up to the customer, then your income will not be the result of salesmanship but rather "buymanship." I'd hate my income to be dependent upon someone's buymanship.

Through observation, experience, and questioning, you can determine what specific results will mean most to your customer. Then you can conduct a sales interview that will be on target.

The preceding examples were aimed primarily toward retail consumers. If you are selling merchandise to a retail dealer, selling raw materials to a manufacturer, or selling equipment and fixtures to a purchasing agent, you will face a totally different set of expected results. A retail dealer is expecting to resell the merchandise at a profit. The manufacturer is considering cost-effectiveness. The purchasing agent is buying the product for someone else. But all three buyers have certain results they expect from the product. The selling process will be the same; only the expected results will be different; that is, the buying motives will be different. Again, you learn which results to stress through observation, experience, and questioning.

Keep in mind that these buyers have their psychological needs as any other customer does; we will discuss these later.

Right now let's examine some of the typical results these buyers might expect:

Higher profits	Faster inventory turnover
Less work	Greater return on investment
Less handling	Lower interest on investment
Lower warehouse costs	Fewer customer complaints
More satisfied customers	Lower manufacturing costs
Less business risk	Product with high salability
Greater cash flow	Business growth capabilities
Fewer service problems	Reduced inventory (similar items)
Less waste or scrap	Less hassle with supplier
Lower service costs	Reduced departmental expense
More referral business	Greater return to shareholders
Product availability	Protection in event of disaster
Reliable delivery	Ability to remain competitive
Volume buying power	Less risk from consumerism

As a salesperson, you should examine each of these expected results in terms of, "How will my product or service produce these and other results for the customer?" If you know your product well and have determined the key results expected by the customer, you are in a position to match them up. Just as with the retail consumer, you must bridge the translation between product features and expected results. Customers are not concerned about the feature so long as they get the results they want. Again, if you want results, sell results.

Let's not overlook the psychological needs of these customers either. Consider the purchasing agent, for example. He wants to look good in the eyes of his management. A wise decision enhances his chances for advancement. He takes pride in making a wise decision and wants to be recognized for it. He will be judged by how well he controls costs, improves profits, reduces work, and speeds up company operations. These factors are important to him from a psychological standpoint, and he considers them carefully as he makes decisions. He is proud of his position and wants to protect it.

The retail businessman, too, has his psychological triggers. He may have an undying urge to be the largest retailer in his area. He may want to be the highest-volume customer his supplier has. He would be proud of being "number one." He may want to expand his inventory in order to be able to advertise the largest selection in the area. Psychologically, he may be competing with a rival retailer for purposes of one-upmanship. He may be domineering enough to try putting the other man out of business. He may simply feel a great sense of achievement in becoming financially successful. He may look forward to the day that he can drive a large impressive car, join the most prestigious country club, or buy his wife a mink coat. That retailer has a lot of psychological needs. The salesperson who recognizes this and aims a sales effort toward both the business needs and the psychological needs is the one who will get the majority of the business. Results are what the buyer wants—business results and psychological results. The salesperson who produces both will produce the most business.

But those results must be the ones perceived by the customer as the really important ones. They are the ones that carry the greatest weight on the "sales scale," the ones that have the most influence on the buying decision. With experience, you will determine the general results most customers seek. Through the effective use of questions and through observation you determine the specific needs of each individual customer. This is the only logical and productive route for the salesperson who truly considers his or her role as a problem solver and a result producer. Such a salesperson has a genuine concern for the welfare of the customer, and the customer recognizes this. It will build a lasting relationship on the basis of mutual interest and trust. It also gives the salesperson an important edge that few competitors will ever achieve.

A fact of business life you have to accept, whether you like it or not, is that the customer doesn't have to buy from you. This is true in all cases, unless you are in a totally monopolistic situation where mere order takers could replace you. Therefore, your objective is to do everything you possibly can, while face to face with the customer, to make him or her *prefer* buying from you. And I use the word *prefer* because he or she doesn't *have* to buy from you.

You can do many things while you are face to face with your customer that will make the customer *want* to buy from you. These include the common business courtesies. But the most important consideration is a genuine concern for your customer, coupled with an honest and sincere desire to help. It is an unselfish concern for the customer, whether you get the immediate sale or not. It may cost you nickels today, but it will produce dollars in the future. Selling is always for the benefit of the customer, not for the benefit of the salesperson.

Fortunately, the vast majority of salespeople I have worked with have a true desire to help their customers succeed. I am proud to count myself among such professional colleagues. If I had no interest in your success, I would never have written this book. It is my sincere wish to sell you on the results these sales techniques can produce for you. It is my objective to make you more valuable to yourself, your customers, your family, your company, and your profession. It is when you have become more valuable to your customer that you have reached the first pinnacle of sales success. And you will become more valuable to your customers when you begin selling in terms of results that are important to them. You should be their problem solver, and when you become their problem solver they can't afford to be without you.

The customer buys the product from which he believes he will get the greatest value; so do you and I. Every one of us has a few selfish motives. I think that everyone in selling would agree, basically, that a customer will buy where he sees the most value (results) for his dollar invested. I have never been able to understand, therefore, why so many people in selling make little effort to help the customer perceive maximum value in a product. They continue to talk about features, features, and features, with no effort whatsoever to help the customer see the results those features could produce for him.

These people have never been able to grasp that buying habits are directed by motives. They have never understood the underlying psychological reasons that salesmanship works. What little success they have had in selling resulted from the laws of predictability or probability—odds. Their basic operating technique is to present their product to enough people, knowing that the laws of probability will produce some sales. Their principal objective soon becomes a constantly increasing number of sales calls per day, again playing the odds. The obsession with increasing the calls per day soon begins to take its toll as the quality of the sales call deteriorates. They don't have the time to help a customer solve his problems. They are too obsessed with getting to the next customer. The odds-players are the kind of people who think you could make a good living selling buggy whips in Detroit—if you just see enough people.

BEGIN AT THE BEGINNING

Results-oriented selling begins the minute you come into contact with a customer. Naturally there are instances where a few social amenities are in order, especially with known customers. But don't waste your time or the customer's time chatting about the weather, the World Series, or fishing conditions. Get down to business as quickly as possible. In a later chapter we will discuss the appropriateness of social amenities, but for now let's assume you are making your first call on a customer. As soon as you have introduced yourself, get down to business.

You will recall that I said you must achieve certain objectives in a logical sequence for a sale to result. Your first objective is to get the customer to hear you out. There is a big difference between the customer who is *willing* to listen to you and the customer who really *wants* to listen to you. Your opening statement should be strong enough to cause the customer to think, "This guy is really worth listening to. I want to hear what he has to say."

For years I have taught salesmen to develop what I call the "traffic cop opening." Here is the imaginary situation I use. Imagine yourself calling on a customer. The minute you walk into his office, the customer puts up his hand like a traffic cop, saying, "Stop! You have exactly sixty seconds to tell me why I should listen to you!" How would you reply to that one? Your opening statement had better be a strong one. You are not going to get very far telling him you have a brand new, jazzy package, or a chrome-plated handle, or nylon bearings in your computerized "franiscanse." He isn't interested that your company has a new research and development department, or that you have increased the dimensions of your "interroceter" by three inches, or that your company has been in business for more than forty years.

Think about the entire approach to selling I have given you up to this point. What is it the customer wants? Results! You had better give that customer a positive result from listening to you. Your objective at this point is not to get the sale. That is the ultimate goal, of course. But right now, your objective, your only objective, is to give the customer a reason to listen to you. If you don't achieve this objective, you can forget about the rest. The customer is asking, "What's in it for me if I spend the time listening to you?" Give him a good positive result he could experience if he listens to you, and he will probably grant you all the time you need for a good sales interview.

Salesmen who call on purchasing agents and salesmen who call on physicians well know the importance of a strong, results-oriented opening statement. Purchasing agents and physicians usually grant a salesman a maximum of fifteen minutes or less to conduct a complete sales interview. That doesn't leave any time for a lot of social chatter. Every salesman, however, should use an opening statement that causes the customer to *want* to hear the rest of the message.

About three years ago I was asked to conduct a special seminar for a group of pharmaceuticals salesmen. Before conducting it, I interviewed more than fifty physicians and pharmacists to find out how they felt about pharmaceuticals salesmen, some of the problems they had with them, how they chose the ones from whom they buy, and a few other pertinent points. A common problem, they reported, is the salesman who spends too much time with idle chatter and doesn't spend his time wisely, giving the physician vital information to use in making a decision. Many physicians said, "Too many salesmen just make a social call, leave some product literature for us to read on our own, and leave, hoping we will prescribe their drugs." Most physicians don't have time to read and digest the mass of literature available in the pharmaceuticals industry. It is up to the salesman to impart the information.

I asked how much time they usually grant for a sales interview, and the physicians reported from five to fifteen minutes. Then I asked, "If a sales representative made an organized presentation, with pertinent information useful to you, would you be willing to grant him more time to give a complete message?" In every case the answer was a resounding "Definitely." There is a message in this, not only for pharmaceuticals salesmen, but for *any* salesman. Any customer will grant you sufficient time if you are giving him meaningful information that will help him, especially in terms of results your product will create for him. In a later chapter I will discuss further information I gained from these interviews with physicians and pharmacists.

Let's compare a typical weak opening statement with one that gives the customer reason to listen. Let's assume that a lubrication salesman is calling on the purchasing agent in a manufacturing plant:

WEAK: "Mr. Conrad, my company has developed a brand new grease that's selling like hot cakes. I'd like a few minutes to tell you about it."

STRONG: "Mr. Conrad, I have a newly developed grease that can cut your lubricant inventory and costs by 40 percent. It also has superior water and heat resistance compared to your two present lubricants. That will give you a lot fewer service problems."

In all probability the purchasing agent would be willing to listen to the first approach, at least for a while. But there's no question about his wanting to hear about a product that could reduce his inventory and costs by 40 percent. From the very outset, the purchasing agent would have a more positive attitude toward the salesman and what he was selling. The salesman would have achieved his first objective: give the customer a reason for listening. This salesman, too, would be granted sufficient time to sell a complete product story and would probably get a sale.

Considering your own product as you develop some strong opening statements, ask yourself a few questions. How will it help your customer? Save him money or time? Reduce his inventory? Increase his sales? Will it increase his efficiency, reduce his workload, or speed up production? Will it give him more enjoyment, more convenience, more peace of mind? Look back through Chapter 2 on "Fundamentals of Motivation" and review the five basic groups of results everyone wants out of life. These will help trigger your thinking as you develop some strong opening statements.

Let's consider some more results-oriented opening statements. Perhaps some could be slightly modified to fit the product or service you sell.

"Mr. Green, in just fifteen minutes, I can show you a way to increase your inventory turnover by almost 5 percent."

"Mr. Edwards, I'd like to show you how I helped the XYZ Company reduce its service costs by 16 percent."

"Mr. Hale, I'd like to show you a new model that seven retailers found increased gross sales by 10 percent in ninety days."

"Ms. Carlyle, would you be interested in decreasing your invoice processing time by one hour each day?"

"Employee theft, Mr. Allen, is a major problem in business. I can show you how to detect and correct it."

"Mr. Williams, I'd like to explain a monitoring system that can reduce your in-line rejections as much as 50 percent."

"Mr. Collins, I would like to demonstrate a new product that has increased our plant production by 10 percent. It may well increase your productivity by an equal amount."

If you give your customer a valid reason to want to hear your message, you have overcome the first hurdle in selling. It sets the stage for the rest of the sales interview and puts your customer in a much more positive frame of mind. The customer will be less resistant and more receptive to your message. Pick out one of the most valuable results your product will produce for the customer and use it in your opening statement. Plan your opening statement well in advance, commit it to memory, and deliver it with enthusiasm every time.

Let me illustrate how an opening statement aimed toward a psychological need opened the door, not only for a sales interview, but also for some rather substantial sales increases. Several years ago, while I was on territory sales in Wyoming, a service station dealer revealed to me a particular goal he wanted to achieve, a new television set for his wife. He was a rather low-volume dealer in a small town and, frankly, felt he couldn't afford a new television set. Before I made my next call on him, I worked out a plan whereby he could get the television set for his wife, essentially at no extra cost.

The next time I called on him I used a results-oriented opening statement he couldn't resist: "George, give me ten minutes and I'll show you a way to get your wife a new television set without any extra cost to you!" His reply was an enthusiastic, "You got it!" I continued, "George, this plan will not only provide that television but will also increase your sales and continue to increase them." This double opening seemed to double his interest and enthusiasm.

Then I explained the plan. I said, "George, looking at your purchase comparison report, I can see that your sales of spark plugs are extremely low. Let me give you a suggestion. From now on, every time you have a customer's car in your bay for servicing, remove the number one spark plug and examine it. If it is clean, put it back. If it is dirty (and about 90 percent of them should be replaced), lay it aside until the customer returns. Show it to your customer and explain that it is costing him in gasoline mileage. Tell your customer you can replace all of his plugs in less than ten minutes while he waits. If the customer objects, tell him he is paying for them in decreased gas mileage anyway so he might as well have the new ones.

Now for the television set. I said, "George, every time a customer buys new plugs, put only the profit from the sale in a coffee can in your safe."

In less than two months George had bought the television set and his sales of spark plugs had increased more than 1,000 percent. A problem-solving approach? Sure it was. A results-oriented opening statement? You bet! A happy, satisfied customer? What do you think? There was another side benefit, too, or I should say a continuing benefit. George's spark plug sales continued at a high level for as long as he was my customer. He got the profits and I got his business. Results-oriented selling works that way every time.

A postscript to George's story gave me some amusement as well as a little pride. I was sitting in his station one day, taking a short break. A competitive salesman dropped in and looked over George's display shelves, which, incidentally, left a lot to be desired. George was never a first-class retail merchandiser, and I learned to live with it. The competitive salesman used a typical sales-oriented opening statement, "George, I notice your spark plug inventory is pretty low. I'd sure like to bring it up to a proper level." George glanced in my direction, winked, and said, "Naw! I don't get that much call for spark plugs around here." What that poor salesman didn't know was that George had my spark plug order written up for me when I arrived. George, his wife, and I had a great steak dinner that evening and a few chuckles.

5

Verifying
Your
Claims

It sure sounds nice when you greet your customer with a dynamic opening statement, such as "Mr. Jarvis, I have a proposal that could increase your return on investment by 20 percent." That should get any prospect's attention. But, brother, you had better be able to prove it. The salesman who speaks with forked tongue is doomed to disaster—and should be.

The next step toward achieving the ultimate goal is the *verification* of our claims. As we continue through the sales interview there are several questions on the customer's mind. The usual, though often unasked, questions that are present in each stage of the sale, shown in Figure 7, are the ones we must answer, in sequence, as we progress through the sales situation.

Salespeople who can verify and prove their claims gain an enormous amount of credibility. Frankly, salespersons should never make a claim they cannot prove. Nebulous or ambiguous sales claims are meaningless, create doubt in the customer's mind, destroy the salesperson's credibility, damage the company's reputation, and make it extremely difficult for

Figure 7. Customer's questions to be answered.

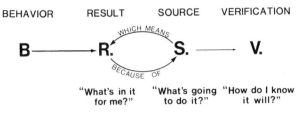

the salesperson ever to call on the customer again. The tragedy of such a practice is the blot it places on the selling profession. Claims that cannot be proved have also created enormous legal problems for sales personnel and their companies. Often, companies have been held legally liable for claims made by their salespeople. Huge court settlements have been made as a result.

I am not so concerned with the legal implications of false claims as I am with the moral aspects. In my opinion, a salesperson has no moral right to make false claims about a product or service. To make such claims serves only dishonest and selfish purposes. In reality, it is no less than lying to a customer. It is a hustler tactic that has no place in professional selling. It is this type of salesperson who creates a negative stereotype in the minds of many people. It is a shame that so many honest and professional salespeople should be the victims of such dishonest practices.

Professional salespeople *want* to produce positive results for their customers. They are convinced that their products can produce those results; they are eager to prove their claims and present information in a sincere and enthusiastic manner.

VERIFICATION STRENGTHENS THE INTERVIEW

A results-oriented opening statement creates interest; a results-oriented interview heightens the interest; and proving your claims intensifies the interest. When you are able to prove your claims about your product, what you are saying to your customer is, "Here's what it will do for you, and here's how I *know* it will do it."

There are many ways of proving your claims as to the results your product or service will provide your prospect. Let's consider several methods you can use to intensify the customer's interest with proof.

Testimonials

A customer would rather listen to another customer than to any sales representative. Your customer may be quite skeptical about your claims but would be receptive to claims made by another buyer. It's a simple case of, "If it will do it for him, maybe it will do it for me." Never be reluctant to ask one of your satisfied customers to give you a letter regarding his or her satisfaction with your product. Most customers are willing to do so unless a company policy prohibits it. At times, however, commercial customers may be unwilling to give you a testimonial for fear you will use it to sell your product to one of their direct competitors. They don't want to strengthen their competition.

A word of caution is in order regarding testimonials. If possible, use local testimonials rather than those from remote locations. A retailer or user in Oregon is not particularly impressed by a testimonial from Florida. Everyone seems to feel that his particular market is different. An Oregon customer will be fairly impressed with any testimonial from the Pacific Northwest, especially from a comparable customer.

Testimonials don't need to be in the form of letters. When you are sitting in a customer's office, trying to verify your claims, it makes a good impression when you say, "Let me give the purchasing agent at XYZ Company a call so he can tell you about the results he got." However, be certain the XYZ purchasing agent has given you permission to use him as a testimonial source. Never use anyone as a testimonial source withour prior consent.

In the testimonials you use, stress results at all times, for example, time savings, reduced costs, better performance, greater profits, and so forth. All your buyer wants is to verify the expected results. To be able to verify your claims adds immeasurably to your credibility. That alone will often close the sale.

Keep your testimonials current. Don't try to use a testimonial letter that is two or three years old. Conditions change, and your customer knows it. Try to keep a file of current testimonials from satisfied customers.

Testimonials, however, can backfire on you, so be careful. If your testimonial is from a customer your prospective buyer respects, it's great. Your buyer, however, has certain competitors he dislikes. A testimonial from such a competitor could possibly create resentment that would cost you a sale. Such a testimonial may be totally unacceptable to your buyer. Before you present the testimonial, try to feel your customer out by learning how he feels about the one who gave you the testimonial. If there seems to be any antagonism, don't use it.

Statistical Surveys

Various published surveys are available for validating certain types of claims. For example, automobile registrations can be used to validate claims regarding top-selling models. In most states, mobile homes or manufactured houses are registered in a similar manner. The best-selling brands and models can easily be identified. When considering his inventory, a retailer can identify those homes that seem to have the best public acceptance.

Industry trade magazines frequently provide statistical surveys regarding manufacture, distribution, and marketing information on various products. These surveys seem to have a high degree of credibility throughout industry. The astute salesman will use this information to verify his claims regarding popularity of his product.

Here is a fine example of using survey results to verify sales claims. Every January, Louisville, Kentucky, hosts the National Manufactured Housing Show. Scores of housing manufacturers and supply companies display the latest models and accessory supplies. Retail manufactured housing dealers by the thousands attend the four-day show to determine which manufacturer they will choose as a supplier, and to select the inventory of homes they wish to sell. One manufacturer posted a large sign next to the front door of a doublewide home, "The number one doublewide in Michigan." Immediately beneath the sign was a Xerox copy of the Michigan Statistical Survey form to prove that this home was the best seller in Michigan.

Individual product manufacturers, too, publish various surveys to show product acceptance, sales ratios, product mix, production levels, and so on. These, too, can be used to substantiate claims made for product popularity. A certain product or model, for example, may constitute 25 percent of total manufacturing for one company, valid proof of product acceptability in the market.

The Product Container

Certain product labels can also be used to substantiate claims. This information may include ingredients, the absence of certain ingredients (no sugar), or recommended use of the product. Motor oil cans, for example, carry label information regarding the type of engine service for which the oil is recommended. Information is also furnished regarding ingredients—detergent dispersant, oxidation inhibitors, corrosion inhibitors, and viscosity index improvers.

Current efforts toward consumerism and truth in advertising seem to lend a certain amount of credibility to information found on product labels. A salesperson should never overlook this information which can help verify claims.

The Product Itself

A wise salesman will always get his customer involved in a product demonstration. If possible, let the customer hold it, manipulate it, disassemble and reassemble it, play with it, and work it. A sales point can quickly be driven home when you tell a customer, "Here, you try it. See how easily that can be adjusted."

Do you remember the earlier example of the appliance salesman who was explaining how the oven door could be removed for ease in cleaning the oven? Let the customer remove the door and replace it to prove how easy it is.

Nothing confirms the comfort of a new mattress like lying on it. Any mattress salesman knows this. For the same reason, the new car salesman wants you to test drive it to get the feel and the handling of it. That makes sales.

Try on a fur coat before a full-length mirror. Spray a new perfume on the wrist. Taste a sample of a new food product. Sit in the reclining chair to see how comfortable it is. Stand in front of the air conditioner floor model and feel the cool breeze. Watch a demonstration of the new microwave oven.

Why do you think these merchants want to get you involved in product demonstrations? It's just good merchandising; it creates sales. Customer involvement is extremely important to any salesperson.

Customer involvement may be more difficult if you are selling an intangible service, but involvement is possible. It is usually handled on an imaginary basis. How often have you heard an insurance agent begin a sentence, "Mr. Burton, just imagine what would happen if. . . ." He may say, "Mr. Williams, let me tell you what happened to a young couple just last month." I have heard some life insurance agents facetiously refer to this involvement technique as "back the hearse up to the door and let 'em smell the flowers." There's nothing unethical about it; it gets the customer involved. Further means of customer involvement will be discussed in a subsequent chapter.

Consumer Magazines

Various consumer magazines publish reports on products that have been tested independently. These reports can be used to substantiate sales claims, and they carry a high degree of credibility. The results of such testing are often used as a basis for advertising claims. They may include tar and nicotine content in cigarettes, microwave oven leakage ratings, gasoline mileage ratings, appliance reliability, product safety, and a host of other information salespeople can use to advantage. Government and nonprofit institutes also conduct such research work (EPA, Underwriters' Laboratories, SAE, ASTM).

Advertising

Although many people view advertising claims with a certain amount of skepticism, you may be able to substantiate claims by referring to the ads. Fortunately, many people have faith in the laws regarding truth in advertising. It's the old belief that it must be true or they wouldn't be able to print it. Those who have studied the field of negotiating refer to it as the power of legitimacy.

Think of the enormous sales volume that results from claims made in advertising. One aspirin goes to work faster than others. A certain tablet has more pain reliever. One is specially buffered to avoid stomach upset. Certain tablets relieve more colds miseries.

Think of the products that put mositure back into your skin. Some products put body back in your hair and make it more manageable. Some products claim to bring faster relief to inflamed tissue. Others relieve itch faster. Still another is proved more effective than the other leading brands.

Other advertising claims include the magazine that is read by more people than any other; the car with the best EPA mileage rating, or the car that has been proved to withstand crashes better; the ball-point pen that is so tough it can be fired from a rifle, through a board, and still write. Or the dishwasher that saves energy; the plastic wrap that won't cling to itself; the insulation that reduces your utility bills; and the luggage that can be thrown around a cage by a gorilla.

If you don't think your purchases are influenced by advertising, you are mistaken. Advertising has a great impact on your thinking, and the advertising experts know it. Salespeople who fail to use their own company's advertising materials are making a big mistake. The power of legitimacy can add substantially to any sales claims.

Company Brochures and Literature

Reams of printed material are available to most sales representatives. These include product specification sheets, construction design charts, photographs, floor plans, flow charts, distribution patterns, testing procedures, construction manuals, application manuals, warranties, guarantees, listings of ingredients, and so forth. The list is almost endless, but all are developed to help salespeople verify their product claims. Although presenting your product in terms of the results it will produce for the customer builds a lot of perceived value in the customer's mind, substantiating those claims with proof intensifies and amplifies that value. It makes closing the sale easier and faster.

Customer Trial

Certain products lend themselves well to customer trial, letting the customer actually use it. An example is the dealer of motor homes or recreational vehicles who invites a prospective customer to take a demonstrator for a weekend, taking the family on a camping trip or to a football game. Some salespeople refer to this technique as the "puppy dog close," that is, take the puppy home and keep it for a week. If, after one week, you're not happy with the puppy, bring it back and you owe nothing. It doesn't require a clinical psychologist to understand how that works, especially after the kids have played with the puppy for a week.

One of the greatest "puppy doggers" that ever lived was the television dealer who would tell a potential buyer, "Some people just can't live with a television set. Let me deliver it to your home, adjust it, and let you use it for one week. If, after one week, you find you don't like television, I'll pick it up and you owe nothing." After enjoying the television for a whole week, who would want to give it up? Or what person is going to let the dealer pick up his television and let the neighbors think it is being repossessed? That dealer actually set national sales records using the puppy dog technique.

On lower-priced products, customers may be given samples to use. This is a fine way to substantiate your claims. In some cases the customer may use a "loaner" for a short period of time, such as a motor home. Think how wise a boat dealer would be in taking you on a Saturday morning fishing or water skiing trip, letting you run the boat under his supervision.

This is the basis for money-back guarantees on many products, for example, "after using X-brand product for ten days, if you are dissatisfied, return the unused portion for a full refund." This is no more than a puppy dog close. Few people will even bother to send back the unused portion, even if dissatisfied with the product. The advertising people know that.

Experience of Other Users

Even in the absence of actual testimonials, relating the experience of other users can be excellent proof of your claims, especially if your credibility has been established with the customer. This is particularly true when your experiences seem reasonable and not outlandish in nature. Then, too, there are certain customers who seem to accept claims at face value and who don't require overwhelming evidence of user success. User success stories are particularly effective when they relate to customers in a comparable type of business. Comparable businesses usually have comparable problems.

Talking in terms of customer results and proving your claims is more important than you may think. It can often bring you a sale even though your competitor's product may be superior in some ways. If the competitor's salesman doesn't talk about it, he might as well not have it. The customer might *infer* that only your product can do the job for him. For example, in selling a house, I might say, "This home has 100 percent copper wiring (feature), which will give you peace of mind as you are sleeping (result), and you can see it right here in this circuit box" (verification). The customer might not be aware that local building codes require copper wire in all new homes. There could be several features that are required by code, and probably are.

I believe in absolute honesty with a customer. If the customer asks whether a certain feature is required by code, I will certainly answer truthfully, but I don't think a salesman is expected to enumerate all the code requirements. To do so would spot every competitive salesman a lot of sales points, and it would neutralize their value as far as my sale is concerned. I don't believe in helping my competitors.

6

Persuasion

Selling without closing is like playing golf without putting. You'll get a lot of exercise, but you won't win anything. For some reason, many salespeople have a psychological hang-up when it comes to closing. Some have such a fear of rejection that they subconsciously think, "If I don't ask him, he can't say no." Such salespeople may do a great job of selling right up to the point of closing and then blow the whole sale at that point. This type of salesperson will usually hint that it would be a good buy, or may indicate that he'd really like to have the business, but will leave the buying decision up to the customer and not push the customer into making a decision. If the customer doesn't buy, the salesman will invariably blame the customer. The art of closing is the ability to state decisions with which the customer will agree. It is not the practice of letting people make their own decisions.

I find it difficult to separate the closing of the sale from the handling of customer objections because these two happen almost simultaneously. For purposes of simplification, however, I will separate them and will discuss closing in Chapter 7.

As shown in Figure 8, persuasion completes our model of the motivational approach to selling, that is, the RSVP sales model of result, source, verification, and persuasion.

At some time during the sales interview, both you and the customer begin to realize that some kind of decision must be made. The sale is nearing a close and something has to happen.

RECOGNIZING BUYING SIGNALS

An industry placard, popular several years ago, stated, "Ten thousand sales were slain today with the jawbone of an ass." One of the toughest disciplines to teach sales personnel is how to recognize buying signals. Some salespeople will sell it and buy it right back because they don't recognize that it is time to stop selling and start closing.

I have often been asked, "When is the best time to close a sale?" The only logical answer I have is, "When the customer is ready to buy." The problem is you don't always know when the customer is ready. Some customers don't transmit any visible buying signals, so the best rule I can give you is to close early, close often, and close late. Keep trying to close, because you don't know for sure which attempt will prove successful.

Research has proved repeatedly that the average sale closes on the seventh attempt. Research further proves that the average salesperson gives up after the second attempt. They are walking away from more business than they are getting because they give up too easily. They seem to take all objections

Figure 8. The RSVP sales model.

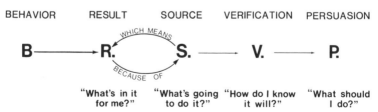

at face value and give up when they could have closed the sale with a little more persistence.

Certain buying signals are as plain as the nose on your face, but others are extremely subtle. The successful salesperson learns to observe customers carefully so as to pick up even the most obscure signals. At times, customers are obvious when they ask, "How soon can I get delivery?" Incidentally, the answer to this one is not a reply; it's a question, "How soon do you *want* delivery?" A customer may ask, "Can I get this in gross lots?" Again, this should be answered with a question, "Do you *want* it in gross lots?"

Any time a customer asks you for something you know he can have, don't ever tell him he can get it. Ask him if he wants it. If he says yes, he's bought it. Stop selling and start writing. Time and time again I have heard salesmen blunder right past this chance to close. The customer asked, "Can I get this in white?" The salesman replied, "Oh sure, I can get it for you in white." There was absolutely no commitment or attempt to close on the spot. If the salesman had asked, "Do you want it in white?" he possibly could have had a sale right there. Don't blunder past this golden opportunity. Close!

Customers who begin asking a series of questions about your product are indicating a high degree of interest. Close! If they weren't interested, they wouldn't be asking questions. They may ask about delivery, terms, methods of payment, methods of packaging, quantity discounts, or warehousing arrangements. These all indicate that the customer is ready to buy. Don't walk by them.

You may notice that the customer has become more relaxed, is less tense, smiles more often. This could be a good indicator that he or she is ready to buy. Try a close.

Of course, an attempted close will often bring up a customer objection. Many salespeople make it a rule to attempt a close as soon as they have answered an objection, simply assuming that the objection was the only thing standing between them and the sale. This is not a bad rule to follow. It works more often than you may realize. Many times the objection really is the only thing standing in the way of your sale. Try it.

Recognizing buying signals is not difficult if you remain observant. Unfortunately, many salespeople are so busy thinking about what they are saying that they ignore not only what the customer says but also the buying signals being transmitted. More will be discussed later regarding closing techniques.

The Mental Chess Game

When the end of the interview nears and both you and the customer realize that a decision will have to be made, you enter into a mental game with the customer. In essence, you have your customer sitting on a fence. I like to call it the "fence of decision." You have put the customer up onto the fence with good salesmanship. You have brought the customer, you hope, to a peak of interest. As decision time comes, both of you realize the customer must come down on the yes or the no side of the fence. Rarely will a customer voluntarily do a swan dive off the fence, come down on the yes side, drop to his knees with money in hand, and ask, "Please, may I have it?"

That customer needs to be *pushed* off the fence—with a good hard close. And I said the customer *needs* to be pushed into a decision for a very good reason. At the point of decision, many logical questions and doubts begin to roll through the customer's mind. An inherent threat factor is present—the threat of a bad decision. This threat factor will be present regardless of your excellent selling efforts.

Some of the questions going through the customer's mind might include: "Can I believe everything this salesman has told me?" "Are the testimonials legitimate?" "Could I get a better deal somewhere else?" "Maybe I should think about this a few days." "Will it foul up my relationship with my other suppliers?" "Do I really need this product?" "Am I being objective about this?" These are perfectly normal questions and should be handled as such. Let's face it, when *you* are the buyer, the same things go through your mind, especially on higher-priced products.

As these questions occur to the customer, the normal reaction is to come down on the no side of the fence and think it over. Don't let that happen. Never again will the customer reach that high peak of interest. The customer doesn't know the product as well as you do and is not the salesman you are. You will never have a better chance to close than when that customer is at that nervous, doubtful, threatening peak of interest. You must push him into a positive decision. He needs your help in making that decision. Give that help.

If you have ever played chess, you know it is a game of "what if?" As you ponder the various optional moves, you continually ask yourself about each, "What if I make this particular move? What options will that give my opponent? What if he moves in a certain way? What options would I gain?" You consider every possible move you could make and determine what options each would give your opponent. You ask the same "what if?" question regarding his options. Then you select the move that is least threatening to you and the most threatening to your opponent and hope you have not overlooked a single "what if?" Obviously, the person who most carefully considers each move, makes the most intelligent moves, and gets in that last devastating move wins. The same is true for selling.

As decision time arrives, the chess game begins. You make a move; it's called a close. Now it's the customer's move; it's called an objection. Then it's your move again. You answer the objection and go for another close. Again, it is your customer's move. You move, he moves, you move, he moves. Just as in chess, the person who plans ahead, considers the options, contemplates the "what if?" and gets in that last move wins.

OBJECTIONS

More important than handling objections and knowing how to answer them is to *accept* them as a normal part of selling.

Don't worry about objections. Don't dread objections. They are as much a natural part of selling as presenting your product. Simply understand them, accept them as normal, and be prepared to handle them in a professional manner. When you and I are buyers, we object, so expect it from your customers. When a customer objects, he's saying, "I'm not quite sold," "I need further information," or "I have a problem which keeps me from buying." The customer is not being arbitrary or ornery or vicious; he's simply afraid he might be making a bad decision.

The purchasing agent is afraid a poor decision might make him look bad in the eyes of his management. The housewife is afraid her husband may feel she should not have committed so much of the family budget. The retailer is afraid the product won't sell well. The physician is afraid the results of the product may prove unsuccessful with his patients. The wholesaler may be afraid his return on investment may be reduced, or that his inventory turnover will decrease. Face up to it; these risks always exist in the mind of the customer. They are normal, so accept them as such.

Objections fall into two categories. First is the legitimate objection, which I define as "a *true* condition which *prohibits* the purchase." Now, please read that definition two or three times. At times, true conditions make it impossible for the customer to buy. That does not necessarily mean the customer won't be able to buy at a later date, but today it may be absolutely impossible. For example, a customer's departmental budget may be so locked in that he cannot buy anything that is not plugged into that budget. Some customers simply cannot afford products or services presented to them by salespeople. Some don't have a current need for the product. Some may not even *want* the product. Some may be so committed to other salesmen they cannot violate that commitment. Some may be bound by national contracts to certain suppliers. Certain objections are legitimate, and you must accept the fact. Perhaps you can't close a sale *now*, but you can certainly lay the groundwork for future sales. Laying the groundwork for future sales is as important as getting today's sales, a fact of life often ignored by salespeople.

Salesmen often accept a legitimate objection as a closed door to future sales and never return. This is a tragic mistake. Conditions change, customers change, and the astute salesman will continue his contacts until that golden day when things change in his favor.

I remember one case in particular where courteous persistence payed off in a big way. I had been calling on a manufacturing plant in Colorado, hoping to gain it as a customer for all the lubricants used in its factory. The plant had signed a contract with a major competitor for its entire lubricant requirements. The prices were competitive, the supply was equally available, and the competitor had a fine line of oils and greases. The contract was renewed on a year-to-year basis, and the customer was completely satisfied with the supplier. It appeared to be an account next to impossible to crack. I felt fortunate to have several such accounts of my own.

I continued to call on the account regularly, and my persistence finally paid off. I made a call just before the expiration of the competitor's contract and caught the customer at a time when he was quite angry over poor service and a misshipment from my competitor. I signed up the account and continued to do a large volume of business until I was promoted out of the territory into a job of greater responsibility. Until the day I signed the account that customer had a legitimate objection; he was bound by contract. Had the competitive salesman continued to take care of the customer, he would have retained the business. The objection ran out, fortunately, when the contract ran out, and I got the business for my company.

The point I am making is that objections are not necessarily permanent. The reasons for not buying today may not exist tomorrow, next month, or next year. Don't turn your back on potential customers just because a legitimate circumstance keeps them from buying today. Hang in there; be persistent but courteous. You may just hit the customer at a time when he is dissatisfied and gain a valuable account.

Your insurance needs today, for example, are not what they were ten, fifteen, or twenty years ago. Your ability to purchase insurance today is quite different from several years ago. Your reasons for refusing insurance agents ten years ago may not even exist today. But the persistent and courteous follow-up by your insurance agent over the years has kept pace with your needs and has kept you adequately covered. Just think of the dangerous position you would be in today if you had not up-dated your homeowners insurance periodically. You may have found yourself in a position of carrying one-fourth of what it would take to rebuild your home were it destroyed by fire. The same might be true of the contents of your home. You may have found that your life insurance program would take care of your family for only a couple of years at today's costs.

I vividly remember the remark made to me by an insurance agent several years ago, after he had looked over my entire insurance package. I thought I had a pretty good amount of coverage. He laid the policies on the coffee table and said, "Well! You don't plan to be dead very long, do you?" I asked what he meant, and he told me I'd have to come back and look after the family. When I analyzed the situation objectively, I realized he was right. My coverage had not kept pace with the rising cost of living. Believe me, I let him correct the situation.

Legitimate objections can block a sale, but that does not make it a permanent situation unless you lack persistence. Later on, as I show you some ways of handling objections, I will discuss what to do about the legitimate ones. But for now, the best advice I can give you is to recognize that objections are temporary barriers. Don't let them defeat you on a permanent basis.

Smoke Screens

The majority of objections you will ever hear are no more than smoke screens. Again, don't take them at face value, and don't worry about them. Accept them as a normal part of selling. They don't necessarily mean you won't get your sale. They only mean you might have to work a little harder for it.

Customers are just like you and me; they put off decisions. Recall for a moment the fears and doubts that go through the customer's mind at the point of decision. Recognize the threat factor present in the customer's mind: the threat of a bad decision. When a customer senses this threat factor, his usual reaction is to get away from it, that is, get away from the necessity of making any decision. The customer thinks that if he throws an objection at you, perhaps you will go away and he will have eliminated the threat.

Rarely will the customer give you the true reason for not buying. Customers are reluctant to admit they are afraid of making a bad decision. Many don't want to hurt your feelings. At times the customer really doesn't know why he isn't ready to buy.

So what does the customer do? He throws a smoke screen at you, hoping you will go away. It would be impossible to list all the smoke screen objections you will hear, but if you have been in selling very long, you have heard most of them. Some of the more common smoke screens may include:

"I want to think about it a while."
"I want to talk to my husband first."
"I want to look around some more."
"It just won't fit our operation."
"I think I can beat the price elsewhere."
"I'm just not sure."
"I really don't need it."
"I'm not interested."
"I'll have to talk to management first."
"My brother-in-law sells one just like it."
"We already have one."
"That's more than I want to spend."
"I don't have enough for a down payment."
"I'm satisfied with what I have now."

Objections Caused by the Salesman

If you will recall, I said earlier that the customer's buying decision will be determined by the value he or she perceives in relation to the price you are asking. Again, value is not in the product; it's in the customer's mind. It is a measure of how much we want something. The goal in selling is to get the customer to *perceive* sufficient value in the results he will get from the product so that he is willing to pay the price in order to get those results. Remember, the behavior you are attempting to get is the signing of the order. If the customer perceives the results as being sufficiently rewarding, you will get that behavior. Behavior is always a means to a result; all behavior is results-oriented. Make the result sufficiently rewarding and the behavior will happen.

This is why it is so important that you always sell in terms of customer results. It is a matter of answering the customer's number one question, "What's in it for me?" The fine features of your product must always be translated into the results they will produce for the buyer. Only results add to the customer's "total perceived value." To repeat, features justify a price but results justify a purchase. The customer's buying decision will be on the basis of the total perceived value. The more you talk results, the higher the perceived value; the higher the perceived value, the quicker the sale closes.

My experience has caused me to conclude that the majority of objections are *caused* by the salesman, either through omission or commission. They result because the salesman failed to do what he should have done, or because he did something he shouldn't have.

Acts of Omission

If you are having trouble in closing, it is probably because you have not yet earned the right to the sale. There are certain things you failed to achieve that would have produced the sale.

Many salespeople fail to establish proper rapport with customers. This is typical of salespeople who are preoccupied with eagerness to get the sale.

The average customer is somewhat apprehensive about being "sold." He may be defensive because of an unfounded stereotype perception of salesmen. Perhaps he is defensive because of an unfavorable experience with a salesman in the past. The salesman who fails to break down this apprehension is making a big mistake. As long as apprehension is present, resistance will continue to build, and the saleman's job is just that much more difficult.

Let me cite a case to illustrate just how this resistance can build in a customer before you even get a chance to talk to him. I am going to use men in this example because I think they are more guilty of this fault than women.

Have you ever taken your wife with you as you were shopping for a new car? If so, I'm willing to bet that on the way to the car agency you thoroughly "briefed" your wife. Your conversation probably went something like this: "Now, honey, please let me do the talking. I know how to handle these salesmen. And for heaven's sake, if you see something you like, don't say a thing to the salesman. You tell me about it." Have you ever done that? Is it any wonder that customers arrive in a thoroughly defensive frame of mind? You can bet your customers have done the same thing. So accept this defensiveness and deal with it to break it down.

As you greet a customer, it is important that you quickly let him know you are there to help him make a proper and wise decision, you are actually on his side of the table, helping him solve a problem, and helping him get the results he wants. Failure to develop this relationship of genuineness, helpfulness, and concern for the customer is a common act of omission among salesmen.

The second most common act of omission is failure to speak in terms of customer results. These salesmen are omitting the one thing that builds total perceived value in the customer's mind, and influences the buying decision. When the salesman tries to close the sale, there just isn't enough weight on the value side of the scale to offset the price side. The salesman hasn't earned the right to the sale and doesn't get it. Salespeople who fail to speak in terms of customer results are wasting the majority of their time and the customer's time. When the customer perceives little value in the product, resistance builds, and objections arise, objections caused by the salesman's act of omission.

Another common act of omission is the failure to use fact-finding questions to uncover the customer's true needs. This keeps the salesman's efforts off target most of the time, and the majority of his efforts are wasted. One cannot apply a solution to a problem that doesn't exist. If selling is to remain on target, one must find the problem through questioning. Admittedly, the customer is not always aware that he has a problem until it is uncovered through questioning. The salesman's failure to use questions creates a formidable barrier. When the salesman's efforts are off target, the customer sees no purpose in buying and resists vigorously.

Another omission in today's business world is a conspicuous absence of common courtesies. I cannot explain this, but it seems that many salespeople feel that common courtesies are unnecessary. They forget or fail to use please, thank you, sir, and madam. They don't bother with follow-up letters or cards to thank a customer for his business. Many fail to make appointments when appointments would provide an advantage. Many fail to thank the secretary who made the appointment possible. Perhaps the worst of all discourtesies is the failure to *listen* to the customer. No salesman has ever lost business because he was courteous. But a lot of business has been lost through discourtesy.

Acts of Commission

Acts of omission are not the only barriers to a sale. There are many things a salesperson may do, usually inadvertently, that are quite counterproductive. These acts of commission usually erode the relationship between the salesperson and the customer. They may cause the customer to like the salesperson a little less or respect him or her a little less.

Smoking, for example, is a common barrier to selling. It is never wise to smoke while selling, even if the customer smokes. Believe it or not, there are smokers who are bothered by the smoke of others. Naturally, the customer won't walk away from you if you smoke, but if your smoke is bothering him, it is distracting and it will be difficult to keep the customer's attention on your sales message.

Distracting mannerisms are also counterproductive and make it difficult for a customer to keep his mind on your sales message. Such mannerisms may include the nervous snapping of a ball-point pen, jangling keys or change in your pocket, scratching, playing with your hair, toe tapping, drumming your fingers on the customer's desk, a nervous twitch, clearing your throat unnecessarily, playing with your necktie or necklace, and so forth. The list is endless, but each of these nervous mannerisms is distracting and will work against your selling efforts. The distraction builds in the customer's mind; he finds them annoying and begins to lose respect for the salesperson. When it comes time to close, the customer may decide he just doesn't want to buy and may not be aware of why he feels this way.

Another violation of professional ethics is the use of profanity in selling. Even the mildest of expletives may cost you a sale. You are never sure of the religious or moral convictions of your customer and the inadvertent dropping of a four-letter word can be costly. A professional salesperson never discusses sex, religion, or politics. Such discussions often lead to disaster and can serve no useful purpose. For the same reason, telling a joke can undo your selling efforts.

Watch your personal hygiene. Brush your teeth, use mouthwash if necessary, bathe regularly, and use an effective deodorant. It is extremely difficult for a customer to pay attention to your sales message when he's trying to keep his head turned away because you have bad breath. Always carry a little spray mist bottle of breath deodorizer and use it just before greeting a customer. It's good insurance.

Dress like a professional if you want to be considered a professional. The type of business you are in will determine what is considered appropriate, and geographic areas have different acceptable codes about attire. Always dress in such a manner that your customers are never uncomfortable around you. No salesman ever lost business because he was well dressed, but a lot of business has been lost by careless or overly casual salesmen. A sales manager once advised me, "If you dress casually, they will take you casually. If you dress professionally, they will take you professionally."

Another common act of commission is the use of terminology with which the customer is unfamiliar. It is easy for a salesperson to take company or industry terms for granted, without realizing that the customer doesn't understand them. Using such terms without explaining them makes the customer feel that the salesperson is trying to impress him with superior knowledge. That builds resentment or confusion and, ultimately, resistance. Speaking to people who are not native to English presents a different but similar problem. I learned my lesson the hard way when I was conducting my first international management seminar in Panama. The group was made up of English-speaking sales managers from various Latin American countries. At the first coffee break, one of the managers handed me a sheet of paper and asked, "Would you please explain these expressions?" I was appalled at what I read. Inadvertently, I had been using expressions which were completely meaningless to the group:

"A ball-park figure."
"We take it out of one pocket and put it in the other."
"He had his head in the sand."
"He didn't know which end was up."
"Who wants to take a shot at this question?"
"We lost him in the confusion."

"Rule of thumb."

"The shoe was on the other foot."

"Twist his arm a little."

"Here's one off the top of my head."

"Another way to skin a cat."

The truth was, I had lost all of them in the confusion. These idioms simply can't be translated. I did my best to eliminate such expressions for the rest of the seminar, but I was only partially successful.

The problem isn't limited to international situations. Language barriers exist here at home between salespeople and customers. The use of abbreviations is perhaps one of the more common offenses: TBA, LCD, LCI, ASTM, HUD, PSI, COE, EPA, SKU, right through the alphabet. The world of abbreviations is often a great source of confusion to customers. Don't use them unless you explain them. The same is true for terminology and jargon used within your company or industry.

If you are selling to a man and wife simultaneously, balance your selling efforts and your questions between them. To do otherwise may lead one of them to feel neglected or to feel you are paying undue attention to the other. The neglected party will be the source of many objections when you try to close. This violation is, perhaps, committed more by salespeople in the real estate business than any other. That is because there's a general feeling that "the woman will make the decision on a house." I question the validity of that statement, but many believe it.

An act of commission that could cause a customer to walk away from you immediately is alcohol on your breath. Some people are so opposed to drinking they will not buy from anyone who drinks, if they know about it. Anyone who comes to work with alcohol on the breath, or under the influence of alcohol (or drugs), should be terminated.

Another problem that has baffled the behaviorists for years

is that some people are reluctant to buy from a salesman who wears sunglasses. For some reason they feel that he is hiding behind them, is perhaps "shifty," dishonest, afraid to look them in the eye. It makes some customers nervous and could create objections at closing time. This is unfortunate, because many people must wear sunglasses, while others simply prefer to wear them.

But all hope is not lost. The behaviorists have solved the problem. If you are one who must wear sunglasses, or simply prefers them, make it a point to take them off a couple of times during the sales interview, look your customer in the eye as you talk to him, and let him know you aren't afraid to come out from behind them. The problem will disappear.

Again, these acts of commission may not immediately cause a customer to walk away from you, but every one of them can become a substantial barrier to your sale. Do your best to avoid every one of them. They have destroyed a lot of business.

HANDLING OBJECTIONS

Whether they are legitimate or a mere smoke screen, objections stand between you and your sale, so they must be dealt with. The better prepared you are in advance, the more professionally and successfully you will be able to handle them. In my opinion, handling objections successfully requires more planning, preparation, and practice than any other selling skill. You must know exactly what you are going to say when the customer resists.

This chapter will give you some guidance on overcoming resistance, but you must determine what you are going to say to the customer. There are no pat answers, even though most books on salesmanship would lead you to think they exist. You must determine the answers that are appropriate for your product, with your kind of customers, and to your style of selling and your personality. What I might say to successfully overcome an objection may not even fit your style. What you might say, on the other hand, may be clumsy for me to use. I might, however, modify your answer so that I would feel more comfortable with it. I would expect you to do the same with answers I may offer.

Although most objections are universally common, especially the smoke screens, there are those particularly pertinent to each product and each industry. You probably know the more common ones in your business. If not, you soon will. I strongly recommend that you take the time to list, in writing, every conceivable objection you think you will ever hear from your customers. Giving each careful thought, write down precisely what you will reply to each, and commit them to memory.

Keep your answers short. The customer doesn't need an oration, only an answer. He's saying, "I'm not ready to buy yet. I need further information to convince me." That means the customer does not yet perceive enough value in the results your product will produce to exchange the price you are asking. It means you must keep selling.

Following is a list of effective steps for overcoming resistance, in other words, the rules for *handling* objections. Later, I will give you some suggestions for *answering* them.

Step number 1. Resist the temptation to jump into the conversation and answer the objection before the customer gets it off his chest. Hear him out to be absolutely certain you know what he is saying. Too many salesmen jump in and start answering before the objection is clearly stated. This discourtesy works against the sale. Hear your customer out. Let him have the satisfaction of getting it off his chest.

Step number 2. This is a step you will never see in any other book on salesmanship, and I feel it is the most productive of all. Never, never, never answer an objection if you can get the customer to self-destruct his own objection, especially if it is a smoke screen. You can get many customers to destroy their own objection by asking one simple question: "Oh?" The minute you ask, "Oh?" the customer will pick up the conversation and continue talking about his objection. If you are patient and continue with, "Oh?" (not in a snide or sarcastic tone), the customer will often talk about the objection until it looks stupid to him. He will often talk himself out of the objection if you let him keep talking. The little question, "Oh?" invites him to keep talking and explaining his own objection. Often he becomes embarrassed at just how unimportant or insignificant the objection is—and buys.

Step number 3. The "Oh?" question will destroy many objections, but if it doesn't, move to the next step, that is, isolate the objection. You isolate the objection with a question such as, "Mr. Simons, I certainly understand how you feel. Is this the only thing standing between you and this decision?" If he says yes, and you can answer the objection satisfactorily, you've got him. He has said, in essence, "If you can overcome this objection, there aren't any more."

Step number 4. Answer the objection. Here is where your advance planning and preparation will pay off. Remember, when a customer objects, he's asking for more information. Put yourself in the customer's shoes and ask yourself, "If I were the customer, what kind of answer would relieve my anxiety about buying?"

Step number 5. Immediately after answering an objection, especially if you have isolated it, go for a close. Assume that the objection was the only thing standing between you and the order. Later we'll discuss closing techniques.

Step number 6. Right after you've gone for a close, shut up! Let the silence become excruciating, if necessary. Don't say a word after you have asked for the business. At this point you don't know what is on the customer's mind. He may be right at the point of accepting and if you open your mouth, you'll blow the whole deal. After you attempt a close, the ball is in the customer's court. Leave it there. If you say anything, you'll take the customer off the hook, bring the ball back into your court, and have to do it all over again. Shut up!

Answer Objections with Empathy

Even though a customer is merely throwing you a smoke screen, he's giving you a reason he is not ready to buy. Try to understand that reason from his standpoint. In all probability his true reason for not buying is completely different from the stated objection. Nonetheless, he has stated an objection and your answer must be given in light of the stated objection.

As we discuss some logical and effective methods of answering objections, I will assume that you listened carefully to the objection, attempted to destroy it with "Oh?" and isolated the objection as the only reason the customer is not ready to buy.

Price Objections

Your price is an easy target for objections. It is easy for a customer to say, "I can get it elsewhere for less money" or "It costs too much" or "That's more than I care to spend" or "That's an awful lot of money." Any way he states it, he's objecting to your price.

There are several ways of approaching a price objection, depending on the type of product you sell and the customers to whom you sell. You might say, "I understand how you feel, Mr. Jones. Other buyers have felt the same way until they weighed the results the product would give them against the price. Have you considered . . . ?" At this point you should restate the product's main features and the results the customer could expect from them. It gives you another chance to build more perceived value in the customer's mind.

You may counter a price objection with a question: "Then you feel that our price is somewhat out of line?" At that point, the customer will probably pick up the conversation and explain why he feels that way. This reflective question invites the customer to talk about the objection. It does the same thing that "Oh?" does. He may talk himself out of the objection.

An excellent technique to use on the customer who says, "It costs too much" is to ask, "How much too much?" If you can get the customer to commit to a figure, you have something you can work with. Your next step is to reduce his figure to its lowest common denominator, that is, in terms of cost per month, cost per week, cost per day, and so on. For example, the difference between an automobile he thinks he can afford and an automobile he really wants might be a thousand dollars. The difference, however, may be only five dollars per week. Five dollars would be a lot easier for him to digest than a thousand dollars.

The American buyer is a strange creature in some ways. The only two numbers the average American buyer can understand are "how much down" and "how much per month." If the buyer can live with those two numbers, he'll buy almost anything. This is especially true for high-priced products where long-term financing is used, anywhere from twenty-four-month contracts to twenty-five-year mortgages. People who sell on long-term contracts or mortgages should be selling in terms of down payment and monthly investment, because the American buyer thinks in monthly terms. He's paid monthly, he pays bills monthly, he budgets monthly, so you should be selling to him in monthly terms.

Price objections usually arise because the salesperson has not built enough total perceived value in the customer's mind. This will be the direct result of selling features rather than selling results. Features build very little value in the customer's mind, and the customer will resist the price. The exchange isn't worth it to him. This is true whether the customer is a retail consumer, a purchasing agent, a retail dealer, or a wholesaler. Perceived value must outweigh the asking price or the sale will not close.

There may be times when a price objection could be handled by putting the customer on the spot with a question such as, "What do you think would be a fair price?" or "How much would you be willing to pay?" or "How far out of line is my price?" You may find that your asking price isn't too far off. In order to get a better price the customer may be willing to make a few concessions regarding such things as free delivery, discount, service, or special packaging. If, however, you are selling on a firm price and have no latitude in price structure, you may have to rely on a restatement of primary features and results. In restating the features and results, be sure to put heavy emphasis on the psychological results the customer can expect, that is, peace of mind, pride, love, sense of achievement, freedom from trouble and worry, and so forth. These will often have a greater appeal than results that appeal to logic only, especially at this point in the interview.

In answering price objections, don't overlook the impact of the "what if you don't" approach. Restate the negative results the customer wants to avoid. Think of the negative results you could stress if you were selling insurance, pharmaceuticals, health care products, automotive services, fire extinguishers, or smoke alarms. You could really put your customer's imagination to work. Be tactful, though.

An example of the "what if you don't" approach is used quite often by insurance agents when faced with a price objection or other objections. They use what is called a "similar situation" to answer the objection. Perhaps you have heard it: "Mr. Wilson, just four months ago I talked to a young couple who also felt the premiums were too expensive for them. I feel terrible that I was unable to help them, because just last month that young father drowned while fishing. His poor widow is expecting a baby soon and doesn't even have a job. That small premium would have left her and the baby protected for life. We all feel it will never happen to us, but we read of these tragedies in the paper every day. Mr. Wilson, that small premium will help your family avoid a similar tragedy. Whom do you want to name as your primary beneficiary?"

Most salesmen, unfortunately, let price objections beat them down. They want to be able to offer the lowest price, the best terms, the fastest delivery, the highest quality, the best packaging. If a product could offer all these, it is questionable whether a salesman would be necessary. Regardless of the product, someone in the marketplace has the highest price of all. Remember, there are many salesmen making a good living selling at the highest price. These salesmen know they must create enough value to offset the price, so they concentrate on the product's features and the results those features will provide for the customer, both logical and psychological results. Having the highest price means you have to do a better selling job. Price cutting is a poor substitute for professional selling. The next time you are tempted to cut a price, remember that every dollar you cut from the price comes directly off the bottom line of the operating statement, dollar for dollar, and out of your commission as well.

Never be ashamed of your price and never be reluctant to tell a customer you believe the price is fair. Stand your ground. "Mr. Allen, we believe in high-quality product at a fair price. That's how we have stayed in business this long. When you compare the value received, I am sure you will agree. What could be more fair than that?"

If you are selling to a wholesaler or retailer, a price objection may be handled with a different approach. The key to a successful product is the turnover rate. If you can validate a high turnover rate, that will usually offset a higher asking price. Some retailers work on a lower profit margin with a higher turnover rate. Others carry a higher profit margin with a lower turnover rate. If your customer is sensitive to turnover, calling his attention to the high turnover rate of your product may tilt the scales in your favor. Just be certain you have the proof material to back up your claim. Your approach may be similar to this: "Mrs. Kinslow, I realize this product is a little higher than some; however, public acceptance has been so strong that it now commands 11 percent of our total production. And remember, that acceptance has been at the retail level where it is really important. Imagine what that acceptance rate could mean to your profit statement."

You are never really sure whether a price objection is legitimate. It could be that the customer really believes the price is too high. It is entirely possible that he has received a lower quote elsewhere. But it may be no more than pure smoke screen. When the customer says your price is too high, ask, "Too high in what respect, sir?" or "Just how do you mean the price is too high, Mr. Wade?" These questions will cause the customer to give you further information, and you may be able to determine whether the objection is legitimate.

When your customer objects to price, in all probability he doesn't understand just what he will be getting for his money. It may require that you review the primary features, results, available service, delivery, dependability, long life, and any particular features that may be exclusive to your product.

If you are selling to a contractor on a bid basis, and the contractor objects to price, be absolutely certain you are quoting identical items in the bid. You must compare packages with your competitor. If you are unable to inspect the competitive bid, go over your entire bid with the contractor to be certain he understands every item included. Don't let the customer compare apples to oranges and then object to the price of apples.

In selling, it is always wise to postpone a price until you are ready for the customer to hear it. This is especially true for higher-priced products. As discussed in a previous chapter, the customer's buying decision will depend on his comparison of price versus the total value he perceives in the product. If the results appear sufficiently rewarding or valuable, he will buy. The customer does not buy because of any single feature but on the total value he perceives, the accumulated value of all the features and the results he can expect from them. Therefore, you want to build his total perception of value as high as possible before quoting a price.

If you give the customer a price at the outset of the sales interview, then he will compare each individual feature against that total price. No single feature is worth the total price, and the customer will retain a negative feeling toward the product. Furthermore, as long as the price is in the customer's mind, he won't hear half of what you are saying. A lot of your selling time will be wasted.

Postponing the price disclosure is not as difficult as it may seem. When the customer asks for the price, you might say, "At the moment, Mr. Miller, I really can't say. we'll have to determine exactly what you need, the quantity, the delivery, any special features, and just what model. As soon as we determine your specific needs, I'll give you an exact price. That way there'll be no misunderstandings. Okay?" If your customer insists on a price and asks, "How much is it as is?" just ask him if he wants it as is. If he says yes, he's bought it. Stop selling and start writing.

Again, there are no pat answers to a price objection. How you handle it will depend on your particular product and the customer to whom you sell. You should determine whether the objection is legitimate or a smoke screen. In any case, however, the customer needs more information that will add to his perception of the product's value. If you build the value high enough, he will buy. Remember, value is not in the product; it's in the customer's mind. Perhaps you can't change the price, but you can change the perceived value of the merchandise. Keep selling.

The Undecided Customer

The undecided customer is one of the most frustrating of all you will meet. During the sales interview he may agree with you, or seem to agree, show considerable interest, and even ask several pertinent questions. You think you have a sale all sewed up until it comes time to close. He stalls, mumbles, scratches his head, and just can't make up his mind. The minute you try to close, he frowns and starts throwing up a smoke screen: "I just don't know" or "I just can't make up my mind" or "I need to think about this a while."

The undecided customer is often a very insecure person. He's afraid of making a wrong decision. He needs reassurance. His objection should be answered with a question, such as,

"Just what part are you unsure about, Mr. Steele?" or "What is it you're undecided about?" or "You seem to hesitate. Just what is it you want to think about?"

Overwhelming proof is what the undecided customer needs. Strong testimonial letters and convincing statistical information provide reassurance. Be patient with this customer and try to instill courage and confidence. Don't confuse him. Treat any new ideas as old accepted practices. Liberal use of the phrase "which as you know" will help build his confidence. Restate the reassuring results your product will provide, particularly those that contribute to his sense of security, suggest a single course of action, and calmly ask for his approval. He needs to be pushed into a decision because he doesn't want to make that decision alone. If he continues to stall, try this question, "Mr. Steele, is there something about your decision-making process I should know that you haven't told me?" It may uncover a hidden objection. If the customer says no, ask, "Then why the hesitation?"

The Shopper

The shopper, the customer who "wants to look around some more," calls for a different approach. Your first objective is to be a "shopper stopper," that is, to destroy his reason for not buying now. Accomplishing this requires asking two key questions. The first is designed to uncover the positive: "Is there anything in particular you're looking for?" If there is something he's looking for, you need to find out what it is. If, however, the customer is just throwing up a smoke screen, he can't commit to this question and he'll reply, "Well, nothing in particular, I just want to look around."

That is time for the second question, which is designed to uncover any negatives: "There must be something about this product you're dissatisfied with. May I ask you what it is?" If there is something he really doesn't like, you need to find out what it is. Then you know what you are dealing with.

If the customer doesn't have an answer to the second question and is still stalling, it's time to stand toe to toe with him and show him what he just did. He's destroyed his reason for not buying. "Mr. Kennedy, you say you're not looking for anything this product doesn't offer, and you say there's nothing about this product you're dissatisfied with. Then it's obvious, this product is right for you. Let's close it!"

This system of questioning will not stop all shoppers, but it will stop a lot of them who might otherwise walk away from you.

"Let's Wait Until Business Gets Better"

Another popular staller is the customer who wants to put off buying until his business gets better. Perhaps he is new in business or economic conditions have forced a slowdown in business. In either case this customer needs to compare the advantages of buying today with the possible disadvantages of waiting. Business doesn't get better; we make it better. Delaying his purchase may mean a higher price later, profit loss, product unavailability, loss of customers, or a reduction in his stock turnover. He would be reassured to learn that comparable customers are buying now. Perhaps you could compromise by offering to sell in smaller quantities until business picks up. Perhaps you could offer extended terms of payment or delayed billing. In all cases, however, it is important that you maintain an attitude of optimism about business conditions. Your attitude will be contagious. Help the customer to see the bright side of things and get his mind off the negatives.

A final clincher you might use on the undecided customer is, "Mr. Barker, every successful company is a monument to its men who said yes."

"I'm Not Really Interested"

Two types of customers say, "I'm not interested." First is the customer who genuinely doesn't want the product, perceives no particular need for it, and doesn't need the product. Let's face it, not everyone needs your product.

The second is the prospect whose favorable attention you failed to get at the outset. If your opening statement isn't strong enough to create at least some degree of interest, it's your fault. Don't blame the customer. It is essential that your opening statement makes the customer *want* to hear what you have to say. If your opening statement doesn't give the customer a reason to listen to you, you've blown the whole deal at the outset. A great salesman once said, "If you don't use the right ten words at the start, you'll never get a chance to use the next ten thousand, or you'll waste them, too." Your first sales objective is to give the customer a reason to hear the rest of your message. If the opening statement is strong enough, you'll seldom hear, "I'm not interested."

I think I can best illustrate this point with an experience I had with a salesman about twenty-five years ago. I had just been promoted from a sales territory to a staff job in Denver, and had signed a mortgage on our first home, which meant I had to buy new draperies, new carpeting, new appliances, and a variety of very inexpensive furniture. Believe me, my budget was committed to the hilt, especially with a wife, two small children, and a mediocre income.

I was working in my front yard, doing my best to scratch in a new bluegrass lawn, when a car stopped in front of the house an a man stepped out with a briefcase in his hand. I was ready to say, "I'm not interested" to anything short of charity. But the salesman's opening statement got my attention immediately and I wanted to hear what that man had to say. He opened with, "Sir, would you be interested in cutting your monthly cash outlay by nearly thirty dollars?" Do you think I would respond with, "I'm not interested"? Not on your life! I laid my rake down and we spent the next half hour sipping coffee and rearranging my finances. He showed me (and sold me) a plan whereby I could purchase a freezer and buy bulk-quantity vegetables and meats at nearly thirty dollars less than I was currently paying per month at the supermarket.

If that salesman had used an opening like this—"Sir, I

would like to show you a home-food and freezer plan that could save you some money," I would have menaced him with my rake and said, "I'm not interested!"

If your customer isn't interested, it is probably because you haven't said anything interesting up to that point. Developing and using strong opening statements will help preclude the negative response. If you hear "I'm not interested" before you get a chance to do any selling, you had better take a hard look at your opening statements. Chances are they are weak and need improving.

If, after you have done a good job of selling, you hear "I'm not interested," counter the objection with, "You mean you're not interested in saving money?" or increasing your inventory turnover, or reducing your work, or whatever the major result is that you are trying to sell. It is difficult for a customer to say no to a question such as, "Mr. Eaton, do you mean you're not interested in making more profit?" Your question will usually draw a response, "Well, yes, I'm interested in more profit. What I really mean is that your price is too high." When your question brings out his true reason for not buying, you'll have an objection you can work with. If you isolate it and answer it, you may well have a sale.

"Leave Me a Price List and Your Brochure"

This could be a classic brush-off, or it might mean that the customer isn't ready to buy today but may consider buying at a later date. Most salesmen have various pieces of literature to leave with a customer. These might include price sheets, promotional brochures, floor-plan layouts, advertising flyers, specification sheets, descriptive material, or product photographs. Unless the customer insists, don't leave the whole package. Ask which pieces would be most helpful, and leave only those. You may not get a sale today, but the materials left with the customer leave the door open for future selling. They give you an excellent reason to return to see if the customer has any questions.

Highlight your materials to call attention to the particular product you are trying to sell. You may wish to mark specific items or information. A paper clip can call attention to appropriate pages. Write your name, address, and phone number on the front of each piece, or staple one of your business cards to each.

Ask your customer if there are other employees who will need to refer to the materials. This could provide the names of various individuals whom you should be contacting.

It is also wise to write up a complete order form on the product you are selling. This brings the information to the bottom line, including price, terms, discounts, taxes, and delivery charges. The only real danger is the possibility that your potential buyer may show it to your competitors in order to gain a more favorable price. Highlighting the primary features of your product may offset this disadvantage, however.

If you have left product literature with a customer, early follow-up is important, by telephone, mail, or in person. It gives you a chance to say, "Mr. Bowers, here is one item I believe I failed to mention the other day." It also gives you an opportunity to see if the customer has any questions he needs answered for clarification. It also lets you know whether he has read the material you left him.

You may prefer to defer his request for literature by saying you have none with you or that new material is being printed. This provides an opportunity to personally deliver the material, thereby gaining another contact with the customer.

If you elect to mail the material, I suggest you mail it in a hand-addressed envelope with no return address on it. This will almost guarantee that the material will be opened, rather than becoming lost among the mass of bulk mail the customer usually receives. If the material is mailed, be sure to follow up about four days later, either in person or by telephone. I suggest you attach this note to the front of mailed brochures: "Mr. Williams, in order to save you some time, I have marked the pertinent information we discussed." Be sure to mark those sections that stress the results your product will produce for the customer. This will focus his attention where you want it, on those things that build perceived value.

When you follow up, either by telephone or in person, the first thing you say should be a *close:* "Mr. Williams, which have you decided on, the model X-36 or the higher-speed X-42?" Or you might use this one: "Mr. Williams, I've checked with our shipping department and we can guarantee delivery next Thursday. Will that be satisfactory?" Many salesmen convey an attitude of doubt by asking, "Mr. Williams, have you had a chance to look over the material I sent you?" Don't ask that question. The customer asked for the material; assume he has read it carefully and is ready to make a decision.

"I'm Not Sure It Will Work for Us"

What this customer is saying in essence is, "Things are different here." Things are different for all businesses, but you must also recognize that your product or service is also different from those of your competitors.

When your prospect says, "I'm not sure it will work for us," reply with the reflective question, "Then you feel things are different in your situation?" This invites the customer to continue explaining why he feels this way. If you can get your customer to explain the differences as he sees them, you are in a better position to explain how your product or service can meet those different needs. If he says only, "Yes, things are different," ask, "In what ways?" Once you have uncovered the differences, direct most of your selling effort to those differences. An effective technique at this point is to get your customer to help you sell by asking him, "How do you think my particular product or service might fit into your operation?" If the customer replies, "I don't think it will," you ask, "Why not?" That puts the ball back into the customer's court, and his further explanation might uncover his real doubts. You can then address those doubts as you continue selling.

"I Buy from a Good Friend"

You probably have some good friends who buy from you, and it's nice to have such friends. But when you encounter the objection, "I buy from a good friend," it sounds like an impermeable barrier, and many salesmen walk away assuming the account cannot be cracked because of the friendship.

Your objective is to disturb the customer's complacency and plant a seed of doubt in his mind. An effective approach is, "Mr. Yates, just six months ago I lost one of my best customers over friendship. We take our friends for granted. I wasn't calling on him often enough, wasn't giving him the service he deserved, and I was spending my time with other customers. I figured I would always have his business, but a competitor of mine showed how he could offer better service, and I lost the account. Mr. Yates, are you sure you're getting everything you deserve from your friend? Perhaps you are, but let me show what I can offer, and then you can be the judge."

Don't take friends who buy from you for granted. Give them the same service you give other buyers. Don't assume that friendship guarantees continuing business.

Answer Objections with Questions

When a customer objects, it is well to find out why he objects. You should find out whether the objection is legitimate or a smoke screen. You also want the customer to continue talking about his objection, perhaps to talk himself out of it or to uncover his real reason for not buying. Questions often can do more than answers, and you could gain some vital information that will give you an advantage in the selling situation.

Following are some typical customer objections and some sales questions in reply:

"I just don't know." "What is it you're in doubt about?"

"I just can't make up my mind." "What point have I left unclear?"

"I'm not ready to buy." "When will you be ready?"

"I already have one." "In what way are they similar?"

"I don't need it." "Why do you feel that way?"

"I'm not ready to change." "What might cause you to think differently?"

"I'm not sure it will work." "If I could show you how it will work for you, would you be ready to buy?"

"No!" "May I ask why?"

"Your price is too high." "With respect to what?"

"I don't get enough calls for it." "Could it be because your customers haven't seen it here?"

"My present inventory is too high." "At your present sales rate, how soon will you have the space available?"

"My inventory doesn't turn fast enough." "What are you doing to promote faster turnover?"

"I have to talk to my husband first." "When would it be convenient for us to talk to him together?"

"I carry too many lines now." "Are they giving you the turnover you really want?"

"It just won't fit our operation." "In what way do you feel your business is different?"

"Our business is different." "Would higher profits give you another important difference?"

"Your delivery is too slow." "What delivery date would be best for you?"

"Can I get it in green?" "Do you want it in green?"

"I hear your quality is bad." "In what respect?"

"I don't buy from door-to-door salesmen." "May I ask why?"

"I don't buy on terms." "Would you prefer to pay cash?"

Questions can be a salesman's best friend. They gain customer involvement; they give the salesman time to think and mentally reorganize; but most important, they gain information that is needed to keep selling on target. Questions uncover true buying motives. They uncover the customer's likes, dislikes, prejudices, biases, feelings, and attitudes. The more the salesman learns about these things, the better position he is in to help the customer satisfy his needs. Questions can quickly turn a sales *presentation* into a sales *interview*, a two-way communication. That's the way professional selling should be.

7

Closing the Sale

Closing the sale is the culmination of the entire marketing process. It is at this point in the process that most salespersons fail. They may do a good job of selling up to this point and then fail to ask for the business. What a waste of effort. Because of the normal doubts in the customer's mind at the point of decision, it is the responsibility of the salesman or saleswoman to push the customer toward a favorable decision. The customer needs that push, followed by reassurance that it was a wise decision.

If you don't have the courage to ask for the business, get out of selling. Otherwise, you are in for a career of rejection and disappointment. Business goes to the salesman who asks for it. You are a salesman; the customer knows you are a salesman; he knows you are after sales; he expects you to ask for the business, so don't disappoint him. Don't waltz around and hint that you would like to have the business. Ask for it. If you don't, you probably won't get it. If the customer doesn't buy, ask for it again, and again, and again. Some customers enjoy making you work for your sale, so earn it. The average sale closes on the seventh try, but the average salesman quits asking after the second attempt. That is one of the primary reasons such salesmen are only *average*. Remember, the average salesman is just as near the bottom as he is the top.

In order to be a successful closer you must *know* you will get the sale. Don't hope, don't wonder; know you will get it. This attitude of expectancy will actually help you get the sale, because it will help you deliver an optimistic, meaningful, and enthusiastic close. If you know you are going to get the sale, the customer also knows he is going to give it to you. It's contagious.

Let's imagine you just landed the biggest sale of your entire career, or had just been given the biggest salary increase of your career. How enthusiastically would you announce the good news to your spouse? Your close should carry that same enthusiasm if it is to have a proper impact on the customer.

WHEN TO CLOSE
When should you try to close a sale? Unfortunately, many salespeople think a close is a separate step at the end of the sales interview. This belief perhaps causes them to put off closing until it is too late. The close, in fact, is an integral part of the sales interview and can come at any time. The close is not something you plan to do at the end of the sales interview, but a close at the right time can *bring* the interview to an end.

The right time to close the sale may be indicated by the customer any time during the interview, when the prospect has reached a decision. These indications may be in the form of questions, actions, expressions, or comments. Don't make the mistake of becoming so absorbed in what you are saying that you miss the customer's signals. Don't sell the product and then buy it right back because you missed a buying signal.

Many customers fail to show obvious buying signals. Therefore, the salesman must use trial closes throughout the sales interview. It is a means of testing customer reaction and may provide some measure of customer interest. You never know which close will work, so you must keep trying. Above all, don't wait until you are finished selling to ask for the business.

If the customer says no at that point, you have nothing left to say except to repeat what you have already said.

Your advance preparation for closing is as important as advance planning for answering objections. You must know in advance exactly what you are going to say. A good closer doesn't rely on just four or five techniques but has dozens of closes ready to use. If you have only seven closes and the customer says no seven times, you are out of business. An excellent rule to follow is to close early, close often, and close late—keep closing. I have often been asked just how long I will keep trying to close a sale. I will try until one of two things happens: either the customer buys, or he can't hear me anymore. J. Douglas Edwards says, "It is better to close too soon and too often than to close too late and too seldom."

Try a close at each of the following points in a sales interview:

Any time a customer indicates an appreciable amount of interest.

Any time a customer begins asking questions about your product. As soon as you answer the question, try a close.

After making a strong point regarding your product.

After overcoming an objection.

When your sales demonstration comes to an end.

When a customer agrees with one of your major points.

When a customer picks up and examines your product literature, the product itself, or the sales contract.

Any time you feel like it.

Rules for Closing

Before discussing a variety of closing techniques, I would like to list my rules for closing sales:

Rule number 1. Ask for the business in no uncertain terms. You are entitled to ask for it, so do it.

Rule number 2. Ask for the business in such a way that it is difficult for the customer to use a blunt no.

Rule number 3. After you ask for the business, shut up! Don't say a single word until your customer responds.

Rule number 4. If the customer doesn't buy, keep selling.

Rule number 5. Reassure the customer who does buy that it was a wise decision.

Rule number 6. Don't stop selling until the customer stops buying. Often a salesman is so elated over one order that he walks away from further business. Perhaps with a little persistence, the customer would have bought more. In the oil business we had a pseudo-acronym, "DOSEQUA SEGAL," which was a facetious way of reminding ourselves, "DOn't SEll QUArts—SEll GALlons." Don't walk away with the sale of one puppy when you could have sold the entire litter.

Rule number 7. Always, always, always thank the customer for the business. The customer should be thanked three times: verbally immediately after the sale, by a follow-up thank-you note within twenty-four hours, and regularly during your contacts with the customer. Business usually goes where it is appreciated.

Remember, in closing a sale it is dangerous to ask for the order in an unplanned manner (see Rule number 2). Some approaches permit the prospect to give you a definite no. The customer who has made a negative decision is obligated to defend that position. Pride may keep the customer from changing. This situation brings up another excellent rule, which may alleviate your anxieties when the customer says no. You can't get a customer to change his mind, but you can get him to make a new decision based on further information. Keep selling!

If the customer gives you a blunt no, meet it with a question, "May I ask why?" That puts the ball back into the customer's court. He will begin explaining why he took a negative stance. That might just uncover his real reason for not buying. If so, you have something to work with and you can keep selling.

HOW TO ASK FOR THE ORDER
There is no one best way to ask for the order and I could not tell you exactly what to say. But there are several methods that

work well in the majority of cases. Naturally, you can modify these examples to fit your personality, your product, and the people to whom you sell. These examples are not original ideas but those gleaned from successful salespeople over the past twenty-five years. These closing techniques have a high degree of success frequency.

I strongly recommend that you develop several typical closes under each style presented, commit them to memory, and use them religiously. Many will work well for you. After you determine those that work best for you, develop several more of the same style. You will be making a costly mistake to venture into the selling world unless you are able to quote at least twenty good, strong closes. You should also set a personal objective of adding one new close to your list every week for as long as you are in selling. The more closes you have and use, the more you will prosper.

Assume He's Bought

You close by indicating that the customer has mentally bought and it's merely a matter of writing up the order. In this case, you don't actually *ask* for the order; just assume you have it. Here are some examples of the assumptive close:

"I'm sure you'll be pleased with the traditional style. I can schedule it in our next production run. Okay?"

"This will start your protection by the first of the month. Will that be soon enough?"

"We can schedule delivery for tomorrow afternoon. Okay?"

"What billing date would be most convenient?"

"Would an initial order of six cases be enough?"

"Will this be the only item you need to balance your inventory?"

"Will you want our crew to install it?"

"Will the larger model be more economical for you?"

"Which shipping method would be best for your receiving department?"

"Would you prefer direct mailing to each of your field managers?"

"By when could you have confirmation from your management?"

"Would you please phone the head nurse and advise her of your decision to prescribe product X?"

"When would it be most convenient to make the installation?"

"By when will you have the financing available?"

"By when will you have warehouse space ready?"

"What do you plan as a down payment?"

"Which model have you decided on?"

"What type of packaging best suits your needs?"

"What type of financing do you prefer?"

"May I phone the order in now?"

"How soon do you plan to move in?

It may seem that I have contradicted my own rules for closing sales, as some of these could be answered with a no. Admittedly, some could; however, I would counter with, "May I ask why?" The customer's response to that question would keep the interview open for further selling, giving an opportunity to use a different close.

Give Him a Minor Choice

Giving the customer a small choice is one of the easiest of all closes to use and seems to be the favorite of most salespeople. A decision on the minor choice is obtained in such a way as to imply or involve a decision on the sale. The customer is given a choice between something and something, never between something and nothing.

"Will you be financing it or paying cash?"

"Would you prefer the three-bedroom or the two-bedroom model?"

"Which would you prefer, the ten-year or the fifteen-year plan?"

"Would you need the twenty-socket set or will the ten be sufficient?"

"Would you rather have the four-door model or the two?"

"Would you prefer it with or without the comfort rest feature?"

"Do you want it in green or white?"

"Which would be more convenient, Thursday or Monday delivery?"

"Which will suit your needs better, individual packaging or the money-saving dozen lots?"

"Would you like thirty-day or sixty-day billing?"

"Which is best for your receiving department, pallet deliveries or bulk?"

"Which is easier for your warehouse to handle, individual containers or cartons of six?

None of these is an actual decision to buy, but the answer implies the purchase. It is easier for the customer to make a minor choice decision than to make a buying decision. Either way he chooses, he's bought. Stop selling and start writing.

Concession or Inducement Close

At times you may have something special to offer to get an immediate decision to buy. This could be merely squeezing the customer's order into a production schedule that is already full, thereby giving fast delivery. It could be offering something extra that is available to anyone who takes immediate advantage of the offer, such as price reduction, special discount, additional features, promotional materials, advertising assistance, display materials, or special premiums. Each of these inducements, however, should be followed with a short assumptive close, such as "When shall I schedule delivery?" or "Which packaging will be most convenient for you?" Here are some examples of concessions or inducements:

"For the next six days, this carries an additional production clearance discount of 3 percent."

"With a gross lot purchase, we will ship FOB your destination."

"Orders taken this week will be delivered next Monday."

"During March, each six-dozen-lot purchase will include this attractive display case."

"During this promotion, for each six cases you purchase, we ship seven."

"For the next sixty days we will provide installation free of charge."

"Until the first of December, a sum equal to 2 percent of your purchases will be provided for advertising purposes."

"With a minimum purchase of two gross, your name will be tagged to our television ads in this area."

"All orders will carry thirty-day price protection."

Again, each of these concessions should be followed with a strong closing statement or question.

Last Chance Close

The last chance close is closely allied to the concession or inducement close. It is used when you can *honestly* state a condition arising in the near future that would make it favorable to buy now. Again, each statement of a last chance situation must be followed by asking for the business:

"Effective June first, we will have a 3 percent price increase."

"The special promotion will end next Monday."

"Effective October first, 11 percent rates will no longer be available."

"The tax advantage will be lost at the first of the year."

"Beginning next week, our delivery schedule will increase to four weeks."

"This is the last week we will offer this advantage."

"Our salespeople will be in this area only two weeks."

"The free sample kits will no longer be available after Monday."

"This program will not be repeated until next spring."

"By the time I call on this area again, the discount will be off."

"It's going to cost you more next month."

"Our stock reduction sale will last only four more days."

"We have another retailer who has been asking to carry our line in this area."

"The advertising breaks on July first, and you don't want an empty shelf when it does."

"This is the last week we're offering price protection."

Let me repeat; never, never, never use a last chance close unless it is absolutely 100 percent true. To do otherwise is not only dishonest but closes the door on any future sales. There is no place in professional selling for dishonesty.

The last chance close quickly develops a sense of urgency and will frequently get an order when normal circumstances would allow a customer to delay a buying decision. Human nature causes us to hate missing out on something. If it will not be available in the future, we want to get it now. Take advantage of every last chance you can, but follow each with a good strong close.

Similar Situation Close

The similar situation or narrative close is outstanding when properly used. Unfortunately, not every salesperson is a skilled storyteller. Almost everyone tries to duplicate the successes of others and avoid their failures. A typical similar situation close, used by insurance salespeople, was mentioned earlier as the "back the hearse up to the door and let 'em smell the flowers" close. All narrative closes, however, don't have to refer to losses someone experienced because they didn't buy. Success stories are equally effective. Following are several that may spark an idea you could use:

"Harold Smith in St. Louis found, by analyzing his sales, that for 101 days in his selling season he did not have a model 70-G in stock. Now he's ordering two at a time and he still runs out before the next production run."

"The XYZ Hardware Store found that moving this item to the prime impulse buying area and increasing the display to a gross lot increased sales 11 percent."

"This particular model accounts for 7 percent of total sales in your own marketing area. If you would like to contact some similar retailers in your area, they'll be glad to verify that. Could I place the calls for you?"

"I presented this same proposal to John Duffy over in Middletown last week, but he decided to think about it until my next call. He called me last night and said he had already missed four sales. That's a $260 loss to John, and I can't do anything about it until I get there week after next."

"Just last month I showed this home to a young couple, but they decided to think the deal over for a couple of weeks. Today a 2 percent increase in interest rates on home mortgages was announced. They probably won't qualify for a mortgage now."

"Look at this article from today's newspaper about a family whose home burned to the ground last night. I tried only last week to get them to increase their homeowner's insurance to bring them in line with today's building costs."

"Last month a retired couple bought this model, completely furnished, and found that their monthly cash outlay was $60 less than the rent they were paying."

"Dr. Lindsey, other physicians have found that prescribing this drug has reduced patient recovery time by two days."

"Most plant managers find that this all-purpose grease can replace three they were using and will do a better job on equipment. That means a 67 percent reduction in inventory and almost the same reduction in operating costs."

"Have you noticed the large number of broken fan belts lying along the highway? Each of them represents a motorist who paid a high towing charge because of failure to carry a spare belt in the trunk."

"Last week I had a call from Ted Syler, a farmer near Martinsburg, thanking me for the fire extinguisher I sold him several months ago. It saved his barn, which caught fire from a short circuit."

As with others, this approach must be followed by a strong closing question or statement. Don't overlook a buyer's desire to emulate the successes of others, or his desire to avoid the losses of others. It's a strong argument for buying now.

Summary Close

In using this effective closing technique, you summarize the primary features you presented and the results they will produce for your customer. It puts the total perceived value back into the customer's mind just before you ask for the order. These results must be in the customer's mind; he must be thinking about them and aware of them at the moment. Otherwise, they weigh nothing on the sales scale as far as your sale is concerned. Review these results, get them back into the customer's mind, and go for the close.

"Mr. Simpson, as I stated earlier, this program will increase your inventory turnover, increase you return on investment, and reduce your warehousing costs by nearly 10 percent. Would shipment next Monday be satisfactory?"

"Mr. Tucker, the permanently bonded finish will eliminate your need for repainting, will be long-lasting, will resist peeling, and will retain its attractive finish. If that's what you want, let's schedule you for Monday's shipment."

"Mr. Jordan, you have seen letters that prove the profit-making potential of this model, that it will meet 60 percent of customer demands, and will reduce your man-hours of labor by 5 percent. In view of these facts, is there any reason to hesitate?"

"Mrs. Kelly, you have seen how our shipment schedule meets your needs, our pallet delivery reduces your workload, and our packaging fits your shipment procedures. Are you ready to improve your profit picture?"

"Ms. Garrett, you see that this new machine can reduce your mail room work by two hours each day and give you a chance to improve your placement of office employees for greater efficiency. Are you ready to take advantage of the gain in office efficiency?"

"Our new delivery schedule can reduce your inventory by 30 percent, and the new packaging system will speed up your warehouse handling by 20 percent. When you consider the current discount rate, aren't you ready to realize all those savings?"

Three-Question Nail-Down Close

The three-question close puts the buyer into an immediate affirmative frame of mind and makes it easier for him to continue saying yes when you ask for the order. To use this technique, you ask the customer three rapid-fire questions to which you know he will agree and then follow up with a simple close. Naturally, the three questions you ask will either be about three points of agreement you had during the sales interview, or they will be based on three points the customer will have to agree to because he has already committed himself—unless he wants to look like an idiot. Here are some examples of the three-question nail down:

"You do want a faster inventory turnover, don't you?"
"Of course."
"You do want a greater return on investment, don't you?"
"Sure."
"You do want to reduce your work, don't you?"
"Yes."
"Statistics prove this product will do it. Let's write it up."

"You are concerned about customer satisfaction, aren't you?"
"Yes."
"You want to reduce customer service costs, don't you?"
"Yes."
"You want to gain referral business, too, don't you?"
"Sure."
"Then let's get this on order now so you can get all three."

"You want to be sure your kids get a college education, don't you?"
"You bet."
"You want their education to continue without interruption, don't you?"
"Sure."
"And you realize that your absence could jeopardize that, don't you?"
"Yes."
"Then let's be certain they get that education, no matter what happens. Let's protect them by approving this plan now."

"Mr. Casey, are you concerned about protecting your present sales volume?"
"Yes."
"Do you want to guarantee your inventory turnover?"
"Sure."
"Do you want to gain a competitive advantage?"

"Naturally."

"Then let's start this program now."

"Mrs. Norman, you want to avoid the rising interest rates, don't you?"

"Yes."

"And you want to reduce your monthly housing costs, don't you?"

"Sure."

"And you want the right house for your family, don't you?"

"Yes."

"This is the home that will give you all three if you buy now. Let's write it up."

The three-question nail down can be used successfully with any product, service, or proposal. Just select three questions to which you are sure the customer will agree, immediately followed by a positive close. If you pick three pertinent points of agreement, your customer will find the offering almost irresistible. If he replies yes to the three questions, he's likely to agree with your request for the order. It is difficult for anyone to reply, yes, yes, yes, followed by no.

Since We Agree That . . .

This close is comparable to the three-question nail-down close. You recall three or so points on which you and the customer agreed, remind him of them, and ask for the order. For example:

"Since we agree that our delivery date is satisfactory, our packaging will reduce your warehouse time, and the terms are suitable, would you please approve this first order?"

"Since we agree that gross lots are more economical for you and our guaranteed return program will protect your investment, let's get the order written up."

"Since we agree that time is your major concern and our shipping schedule will meet it at a competitive price, may I phone the order in right now?"

"Since we agree that your present turnover rate means you will need delivery in thirty days, may I get this order scheduled into our production line today?"

This technique refocuses the customer's attention on certain items on which agreement had been reached during the interview. It also takes his mind away from points of disagreement or concern that may cause resistance.

Keep One in the Briefcase

It is an excellent idea to hold back at least one good product feature that you might need as a clincher if all else fails. Many tough accounts have been gained with this technique.

There comes a time in any sales interview when it is apparent to both the customer and the salesman that the salesman should leave. At this point the salesman starts putting all his materials back into his briefcase. Thinking the salesman is on his way out, the customer drops his defenses. While the defenses are down, if the salesman has held back one outstanding product feature, there's a good chance he can close a sale by selling that feature's result. He might turn to the customer and try a close such as:

"Mr. Martin, isn't it possible that our oxidation inhibitor could prevent a lot of your present customer complaints?"

"Mr. Sellers, would lubrication-free sealed bearings help reduce your maintenance costs?"

"Mrs. Julian, would our one-year free service contract alleviate your concerns?"

"Mr. Carson, since freight costs are one of your concerns, would sharing a drop shipment with another buyer be of any help?"

These questions may well open the door for further selling, giving you an opportunity to restate some of your primary features and go for an additional sale.

OTHER CLOSING TECHNIQUES

No matter what close you attempt, let there be no doubt that you are asking for the business. Don't hint around that you would like to have the business; ask for it.

One of my favorites is a simple, "Let's close it!" Another of my most effective is to extend my hand for a handshake and ask, "Do we have a firm deal?" Others may include, "Let's wrap it up," "Let's get the order filled out," "Let's get it in the production schedule right now," "Let me phone the order in for you," and "Let's get it written up."

There is absolutely nothing wrong with, "Mr. Skelton, may I have your business?" Frankness and sincerity will accomplish your objective more effectively than cleverness.

Don't waltz with a customer when it comes time to close. Ask for the business in no uncertain terms. Here are some of the typical waltzes often heard:

"I sure would like to ship you one of these."
"I think you'll be making a mistake if you don't buy."
"This will be a real good deal for you.'
"You can see what this plan will do for you."
"This is one of our best sellers, and it will work for you."
"This will sure make you a bunch of money."
"You shouldn't pass up a deal like this."
"This is a real sharp model."

These are not closes at all, just laudatory statements. Remember, you do not have a close until you have put the ball squarely into the customer's court and he is *required* to make the next move.

Regardless of what close you use, if you get the order, there is still one more close that must be used every time: "Is there anything more I can get (order) for you?" Don't stop selling until the customer stops buying.

Every good salesperson gets turned down occasionally, but the difference between the outstanding salesperson and the average one is that the former always bounces back and tries, tries, and tries again—never less than seven times. If you want to be successful at selling, make this "rule of seven" a part of your professional life. It pays big dividends.

8

Know Your Customer

This chapter will deal with two types of salespeople: those who call on customers on the basis of repeat business and those who call cold almost entirely. Neither type of selling is more important than the other, just different. Therefore, I will discuss them separately, although it would be well for both types of salespeople to study this entire chapter carefully. There are ideas in each section that will help either type.

REPEAT BUSINESS

If you are in a business dependent upon calls to existing customers and new prospects, it is essential that you know as much as possible about each. This is important, not just to give you an advantage in the selling situation, but so you will be more valuable to your customers. The more you know about your customer, the more you are in a position to help him grow and prosper in his particular business. Most salespeople feel they are responsible *for* the customers in their territory, but few perceive themselves as being responsible *to* their customers. This is a perspective that every successful sales representative must develop.

A personal friend of mine, Zig Ziglar of Dallas, Texas, put this concept into the right perspective when he said, in essence, "You can get anything you want out of life if you will just help enough other people get what they want out of life."* This is a fact of life in selling. One of your greatest responsibilities is to see that your customers succeed in their individual businesses. Your product or service is a means of helping them prosper, grow, and succeed.

In any business relationship there are three principals, namely, the company, the salesperson, and the customer. For a moment, imagine these three principals, each at one point of a triangle. Without exception, each is entitled to profit from a sales transaction in some way. Each is entitled to certain *results* from the transaction. From this standpoint, you, as the salesperson, are serving three worlds, each with different values.

Your company is entitled to a fair profit, good relationships, freedom from worries or hassles, a favorable reputation, and future opportunities for repeat business.

You are entitled to a fair commission or income, a lasting relationship, courteous treatment, and the opportunity to return for further selling.

The customer is entitled to results from the product or service, results that will enhance his success, growth, or satisfaction.

It is important that you approach every selling situation with this triangle in mind. Unfortunately, many salespeople approach each sales situation from a selfish standpoint, concerned only with their own income, with little regard for the welfare of the customer or the company—and they wonder why they have trouble gaining repeat business. When all three parties gain from a sales transaction, it is a healthy transaction and will invariably lead to repeat business, the foundation upon which a successful sales territory is built.

* Zig Ziglar, *See You at the Top*. Gretna, La.: Pelican Publishing Co., 1977.

This concept was put into proper perspective by a young petrochemicals sales manager who attended one of my management seminars in Singapore. He said,"My main objective is to put together a deal where my company and my customer will write each other a thank-you letter. When that happens, I have succeeded."

Your product or service will produce positive results for your customer. That is the basis on which you sell it. Presenting these results to your customer is the heart of the sales interview. Your job is to succeed by showing others how to succeed through using or selling your company's products.

Previous chapters discussed the importance of learning to "read" your customer, the importance of asking questions to determine the results that would be most important to the customer. Only when you know the kind of results the customer expects are you in a position to keep your selling on target. Only then can you determine which product or service will produce the desired result for the customer. Without this knowledge it would be virtually impossible for you to follow the concept of the RSVP sales model. It is vital that you learn which results your customer seeks. What are the positive results your product or service can provide him and what are the negative results you can help him avoid? The more you know about your customer, the more you are able to keep the selling process going in the right direction.

The longer you are in the territory and the more times you call on any given customer, the more you will know about him and the more you will understand his motivational triggers. But don't rely on memory and luck to develop this vital information. Go after it in a logical, planned manner, and record every bit of information as you get it. This chapter will help you develop a strategy for gaining and recording the information you need.

Customers have many different kinds of personalities. Each is a complex mechanism of reason and emotion, motivated by a multiplicity of impulses. Each requires special consideration and attention. Ways of appealing to customer motives will vary, as we discussed in the chapter on "Fundamentals of Motivation." No two customers are alike; therefore, there is no pat way of dealing with them.

Obviously, then, the salesperson should know everything possible about each customer. This requires some method of gaining and keeping information up to date and handy for everyday use. Many salespeople keep a permanent customer record file in the form of a loose-leaf notebook as a ready reference. Others keep a card file.

Whatever system you use should contain all vital information that will give you an advantage in a selling situation. It should contain the names of all persons who can buy or influence buying, all facts that could be of value to you in preparing a sales plan, all information you can gain regarding the customer's personality and motivational profile. It should contain all information you can gather that will help you bridge the conversational gap between the usual social amenities and the serious sales conversation. The best method I have found for gathering and recording this information is the Confidential Account Diary shown in Figure 9.

The Confidential Account Diary is for *your* use only and the word *confidential* must be taken seriously. Much of the information you enter will be subjective in nature. The three-ring binder holding your diaries should be kept locked in the glove compartment of your car for review just before you make a sales call. Never carry it in your briefcase. You may accidentally leave your briefcase in a customer's office, and the subjective information in the diary could create unwanted complications for you. You could even encounter some legal entanglements.

While on a sales territory, I kept all customer information in a three-ring binder with two sets of alphabetical tabs. The first set of tabs indicated account locations. For example, if I drove into North Platte, Nebraska, I would go to the N tab and find North Platte. On one sheet there was a listing of every account

I had in North Platte. Let's assume I wanted to call on the Apex Oil Company there. Under the second set of tabs I would locate the Confidential Account Diary for Apex. There I found a wealth of information to help me approach the account in an intelligent manner. I had personal information on the customer that put us on a common ground quickly and helped me establish immediate rapport. If the customer liked to talk about fishing, I knew that. If he objected to drinking, I knew that. If this date happened to be his birthday, or anniversary, I knew that. If he was prone to argue with salesmen, I knew that. Fortunately, the salesman whom I replaced on the territory handed me a nearly complete set of diaries on all his accounts. They were invaluable in helping me get off to a successful start in the territory. In time, all were passed on to my successor.

Gathering the information for the diary takes a lot of time, but eventually you can get all the information you need. During each sales call, bits of information will drop, such as birthdays, anniversaries, and so forth. A couple of well-posed questions will gain more information; however, don't subject your customer to a personal interrogation.

The diary also serves as a red flag for those little things you don't dare overlook. For example, let's say I called on the Apex Oil Company and was told by the receptionist, "I'm sorry, Mr. Dillard can't see you today. He's at the hospital with his wife; she just had a knee operation." I would make a note of this on bright red paper and attach it to the front of the Apex diary as a reminder. My opening statement on my next call on Mr. Dillard, of course, would be, "How's Mrs. Dillard?" If, however, I knew the customer well enough, Mrs. Dillard would receive flowers in the hospital, along with a get-well card. This, of course, is a discretionary matter depending on your knowledge of the customer.

The diary helps you remember birthdays and anniversaries. The salesman who remembers these little things has a great advantage over a competitor who pays no attention to them.

Figure 9. Confidential Account Diary.

CONFIDENTIAL *Account Diary*

Much of this information is subjective in nature, based on opinions — BE CAREFUL!

Name of Dealership: _____

Address: _____ Phone: _____

Dealer's Name: _____ Nickname: _____

Sales Manager: _____ Nickname: _____

Secretary: _____ Nickname: _____

Service Manager: _____ Nickname: _____

Who Controls the Buying? _____

Best Time to Call: _____

Information On The Dealer

Age: _____ Birthday: _____ Wedding Anniversary: _____

Where is He From, Originally? _____

How Long in Business? _____ Previous Business: _____

Military Information: _____

College Information: _____

Civic Organizations: _____

Hobbies: _____

What Does He Like to Talk About? _____

Does He Drink? _____ What Does He Drink? _____

Does He Smoke? _____ What Brand? _____

Wife's Name: _____ Number of Children: _____

Names of Children (ages) _____

Describe His Personality: _____

_____

Describe Your Business Relationship With Him: _____

_____

_____

What Are His Business Plans? _____

_____

What Type of Promotions Does He Run? _____

_____

_____

What Type of Advertising Does He Do? _____

_____

_____

Any Regular Problems With Him? _____

_____

How is He Best Handled? _____

_____

_____

Does He Have Any Perpetual Gripes? _____

_____

What "Turns Him On" From A Motivational Standpoint? _____

_____

_____

What Trophies, Plaques, Pictures, etc. Are in His Office? _____

_____

Any Idiosyncrasies, Unusual Habits or Prejudices? _____

_____

Other Information Which Would Help in Handling This Account: _____

_____

_____

_____

_____

_____

_____

_____

_____

But there are many things other than birthdays that should be remembered. Customer idiosyncrasies, attitudes, prejudices, likes, dislikes, and motivational triggers provide many keys to selling him. You know which subjects to bring up and you know which to avoid. You can keep the sales conversation channeled into productive directions. You are in a better position to keep your customer in an affirmative frame of mind, an important sales technique that will be discussed in Chapter 13.

A thorough knowledge of the customer is vital in every phase of the RSVP sales model. You have a more thorough understanding of the results he seeks, both logically and psychologically. You can better determine which of your product features is the source of those results. You will know which means of verification will be most credible, and you will know which means of persuasion will be most effective. Knowledge of the customer is vital to each step in the RSVP selling process.

CALLING ON PROSPECTS
Calling on prospects, however, may be an entirely different situation. On-the-spot judgments may have to be made. Earlier we discussed the importance of making a quick cursory analysis of the customer's office to determine the type of image he is trying to project. What he wears, how he talks, what he displays on his walls and bookshelves are all clues to the image he wants you to see. These items may help you size him up and help you get into a more productive sales dialog with him, but you still have to deal with his basic personality. Dealing with various customer personalities is one of the great challenges of selling. Let's examine a few.

Can't Make Up His Mind
In the chapter on handling objections we discussed the undecided customer and some of the things you could do to bring him to a logical decision. This is usually an insecure person

who needs a lot of convincing. He needs overwhelming evidence that your product will help him. He is impressed with success stories and strong testimonials from other buyers. He needs a lot of reassurance that a favorable buying decision would be wise. His attitude is definitely yes, maybe. He seems to agree with you throughout the sales interview, but when it comes time to make a decision, he balks, falters, and starts throwing out objections to avoid making a decision. He is sensitive and will resent any implication that he doesn't know his own mind.

Be patient with him, present strong supporting evidence, point out one course of action you want him to take, and assume he is in agreement with you. Frequent use of the phrase "which as you know" throughout the interview will bolster his self-confidence. Your close should include a thought such as this: "Mr. Jenkins, your decision to buy certainly indicates your knowledge of the field," or "Mr. Jenkins, your management will certainly see the wisdom in your decision to buy now." He needs assurance that a buying decision is wise. Give it to him.

The Know-It-All

This guy is determined, convinced he knows all the answers, and is the complete opposite of the customer who can't seem to make up his mind. Many salespeople will avoid this customer because he tries to make them seem incompetent and uninformed. He is the authority and wants you to know it. Actually, your chance of selling him is improved because many salespeople stay away from him. If you are patient and know how to deal with him, you can sell him.

Don't try to push this customer too hard and don't make your suggestions too positive. He likes to talk, so guide the entire sales interview with *questions*. You must listen to him and indicate a strong interest in what he says. Even if he is incorrect in what he says, never contradict him. Ask about his interests, his business, his plans, his ideas, and ask for his suggestions. A great question for this customer is, "What do you think would be best in this situation?" Frankly, he's dying to tell you.

Your questions will guide him through your entire sales interview if you plan carefully. What you must do is allow him to sell himself. Inject a few thoughts into the conversation, and he will seize upon them as his own. Be sure to concentrate your end of the conversation on the results your product will create for him, liberally spashed with "which as you know." This customer doesn't want you to ask for the order as much as he wants to give it to you. He wants to be the decision maker, so let him be. A close such as this should prove effective on the know-it-all: "Mr. Allen, with your extensive knowledge of this product and what it will do for you, what is your decision regarding shipping date?"

Let's Be Friends

This customer is more of a socialite than he is a businessman. He would rather visit than buy, he always enjoys having someone to talk to, and he is a great conversationalist over an expense account dinner. One of the problems you face with this type of customer is keeping his mind on your sales information. He will steer the conversation away from selling at every opportunity, and it will be necessary for you to get him back on the right track. One good method is to use pertinent questions. Another is to keep something tangible in front of him, such as brochures, samples, literature, or the product itself. These focus his attention on what you are saying.

This customer can be frustrating. He will be agreeable, will raise few objections, and is quite likely to sidestep the issue of signing an order. You will need to use as many trial closes as possible and watch for every opportunity to close. Rather than ask for the business in so many words, it would be well to write up the order, hand it to him with a pen, and say, "Mr. Vickers, would you please okay this for me?"

The Antagonist

Although this customer is obnoxious, he can be a great source of business, because most salespeople will avoid him. He is an arguer, seems impossible to deal with, and will beat a salesman down at every opportunity. In many ways he must be handled similar to the know-it-all customer. You have to make him think that every idea is his and that he is the authority.

During your product presentation he may show no apparent interest whatever. He loves to object just to antagonize you. He may complain about your product, your company, or even you. Be patient. Let him play his little game. In no way should you display any discomfort because of his lack of interest. Be businesslike in every respect and try to make it appear that you like and respect him. For the volume of business you can extract from him, you can afford to take some guff.

As he talks, interweave the merits of your proposition into his conversation. Show him that what you sell will help him achieve the results he seeks, and check your progress with an occasional question. Keep on selling as long as he will listen. Remember, he's going to buy from someone, and he is just making you earn your sale.

Old Zipper-Lip

One of the most frustrating prospects is the one who won't say a thing. It is difficult to check your progress with this person. You don't know what is on his mind, you don't know whether he is in agreement with you, and you may question whether he is even listening.

The most effective means of drawing this customer out is the liberal use of open-end questions, those that cannot be answered with a yes or no. The most effective questions are those that begin with, "Mr. Rogers, what do you think about . . . ? How do you feel about . . . ? What is your opinion concerning . . . ?" If you are unable to get any response from him, and it will often happen, I suggest you ask a very blunt question: "Mr. Rogers, would you mind telling me what the hell's on your mind?" I do not believe in the use of profanity in selling, with this one frustrating exception. I feel that a little shock therapy can be a great ally at times.

If you are one who has studied body language, it could be your salvation with this customer. The minute you see an agreeable posture, go for a close. If you see a distant posture, avoid a close. You must catch him at the right moment and use a strong, positive close. Your own body language can influence the customer, too, so maintain a positive posture at a proper and safe distance.

In dealing with any type of customer, remember that there is always a key to the situation to be found somewhere. It will be necessary for you to be flexible in all situations. You must adjust to the personality of the customer so as to gain and maintain the most favorable rapport. Accept each customer as he is, understand him, and deal with him accordingly. The salesman who does will be successful in most cases. All prospects must buy from someone. Why shouldn't it be you?

YOUR RESPONSIBILITY

As the territory sales representative, you are responsible for knowing more about that territory and the people in it than any other person in your organization, if not now—soon. It is your responsibility to gather as much customer information as possible, information that will give you an advantage in the sales situation. Further, it is your responsibilty to record as much customer information as possible in the Confidential Account Diary, not only for your own use, but to pass on to your successor.

Your responsibility goes beyond selling, too. You are expected to help each customer to the point where complaints, inquiries, orders, invoices, claims, and service/parts requests are handled to the customer's satisfaction. It is important, however, that you maintain a strong balance of loyalty between your customer and your company, never compromising one at the expense of the other. There are times when you must say no to a customer's request for something you know you can't do. There will be times when you must go to your management and fight for something for your customer because you know it is right. You will be serving two worlds, company and customer, and you have responsibilities to each.

You should know as much as possible about your customer, including his plans for expansion, business growth, and his potential problems. You should keep abreast of any potential regulation or legislation that might have a bearing on his business. You should keep abreast of business finance and trends in interest rates. Interest rates may affect the customer's plans for capital expenditures for expansion or inventory buildup.

You are expected to maintain the kind of business relationship and customer acceptance that will enable you to penetrate the account and reduce competition to a minimum. In order to do this, you must know as much as possible about that customer, for example:

Who is the business owner?
Who controls the buying?
Who influences the buying?
Who runs the business?
What brands does he carry?
What is his sales volume?
Who is responsible for operations?
In what quantities are products used?
Are there seasonal trends?
What are his plans for expansion?
What problems does he face?
What is his relationship with other suppliers?
What is the condition of his operating equipment?
What are his buying habits and patterns?
What are his purchasing procedures?
What are his financing procedures?

How does he pay?
What are his merchandising procedures?
Does he advertise?
Is he promotion-minded?
Where can I help him with his plans?

Always remember, the customer doesn't *have* to buy from you, but there are many things you can do that will give the customer a reason to *prefer* buying from you. If you can help your customer grow and prosper, you are of great value to him. It will give you an important edge over your competition. The more you know about his business, the more valuable you will be to him, and he knows it.

If you sell products to either wholesalers or retailers, there is another area where you can be of value to your customers: training *them* in methods of selling your product. Your objective should not be one of selling *to* your customer, but rather one of selling *through* your customer. If you can help him unload his shelves, empty his stockroom, or increase his inventory turnover, then restocking becomes extremely easy for you. Any retailer would prefer doing business with a salesperson who can help him sell more. The majority of my sales experience has been in selling to distributors and retailers, and helping them to increase their sales was always one of my primary objectives. When their sales volume increased, my volume increased.

Your sales interview is conducted usually with the retailer. Don't overlook the people who will be reselling the product for him. Take the time to discuss the product with them. Show them your primary product features and tell them how to present them to customers in terms of results. Tell them how to handle customer objections and questions. If possible, conduct a little role-playing session with these salespeople. It will build their self-confidence toward selling your product and will pay off handsomely for you and your customer.

THE COLD CALL

There are many people in selling who do not rely to any extent on repeat business. In essence, every call is a cold call. Even with salespeople who depend on repeat business, many of their prospect calls are cold calls.

In *any* cold call, I sincerely believe the most important part of the entire sales interview is the opening statement. I think it would be well for you to reread the information on the "traffic cop opening" in Chapter 4. Your opening statements will have a direct bearing on the number of sales interviews you will be able to conduct.

Many cold calls on prospects begin with a receptionist or secretary. Your first objective is to get an *appointment* with the prospect, and the receptionist or secretary will determine whether you ever get one. She is your first selling job, that is, selling her on giving you an appointment.

That secretary's job is *not* to keep salesman out. Her job is to *screen* salesmen, and let in only those who have something worthy of hearing. Your opening statement to her is just as important as your opening statement to her boss. The question on her mind is, "Why should I let you talk to him? What's in it for him?" If you can make your proposition seem sufficiently valuable to *him*, she will give you an appointment.

Put yourself in the secretary's place and decide which of the following statements would cause you to give a salesperson an appointment:

"Miss Cameron, I'd like to talk to Mr. Snyder about a brand new inventory control system my company has come out with, a system that just might save him some money."

"Miss Cameron, I represent a new method of controlling warehouse inventories that customers report has reduced their man-hours by 20 percent and speeds up shipping by one full day. I'd like to show Mr. Snyder how he can enjoy those savings. When may I have fifteen minutes with him?"

In the first statement there was an *implied* customer outcome or result. The second, however, stated two specific results the salesperson could produce for the buyer. The latter also had a "close." The secretary would more likely grant an interview for the second statement. It would be her responsibility to bring in a proposal that could produce such results for her boss. That is the kind of sales interview she is expected to grant. At the very outset you must give the secretary or receptionist a *reason* to grant you an appointment. If you carefully plan your opening statement to her, you usually will get an appointment. Sell the secretary, or you will never get a chance to sell the boss.

Don't try to be "cute" with a secretary, and never use subterfuge as a means of getting by her. Be honest with her. Subterfuge may get you through the door the first time, but that is likely to be your last. The common use of subterfuge is one reason that many secretaries (and customers) have become anti-salespeople.

A subterfuge that irritated me occurred in my own neighborhood. A home just four houses from mine was sold to its second owner. On a bright Sunday afternoon, a well-dressed man in his mid-thirties appeared at my front door. He introduced himself as the new neighbor and said he just wanted to drop by, to get acquainted with his new neighbors, and to learn something about the neighborhood. Naturally, I was delighted to welcome him into my home. For the next thirty minutes he asked about the other neighbors, who they were, their names, where they worked, number of children, and so forth. He implied that he might plan a lawn party to get better acquainted. Frankly, I thought it was great until he finally stated his real reason for being there.

He said, "Mr. Evered, I'm the agent for the XYZ Life Insurance Company, and I would like to go over your insurance program while I'm here to see whether there are any gaps in it I can fill."

It didn't take me long to get rid of him, and the only time I have seen him since is when he drives by my house on his way home. Furthermore, I don't ever want to see him again. Not only did he disrupt a Sunday afternoon for me but he used subterfuge to get into my home. Not only would I refuse to buy from him but it's doubtful that he will ever get any business in the neighborhood. I made a point of telling the neighbors how he got in.

This is not to be taken as an indictment of insurance agents, only an indictment of the method used by this one to get through my door. Had he been honest with me (but not on Sunday), told me what he wanted, and done so in a businesslike manner, chances are he would have been able to visit me regarding insurance. I would have been in a receptive frame of mine. He mailed company brochures to me, but that stopped after I marked a couple of them "refused" and stuck them into his mailbox. I admire any salesman who goes after business, but not on the basis of subterfuge.

Just recently, a family friend cited another incident of subterfuge. An evening telephone sales call came from a company offering an excellent spot remover, to be used on either carpeting or upholstery. The salesman asked for an appointment to demonstrate the product. Having two or three critical spots that needed removing, my friend granted an appointment for the following evening. At it turned out, the spot remover was used only as a means of gaining entry into her home. The salesman showed up with a vacuum cleaner under his arm. He never made it through the door.

Even for the door-to-door salesperson, the opening statement is the most important part of the sale. It will determine whether you even get through the door. Again, no subterfuge. Just plan a series of results-oriented opening statements and use them with sincerity, enthusiasm, and honesty. If you are selling a reliable product that will provide some worthy results, you will have no reason to use subterfuge. If you are getting a lot of doors slammed in your face, it's probably because you aren't giving people a good reason to let you in.

I recall years ago having many doors slammed in my face.

Although I didn't realize at the time why it was happening, I now know why. My opening statements were not giving people a valid reason for letting me in or for listening to me. Needless to say, I wasn't too successful in my door-to-door insurance selling.

A later venture in door-to-door selling proved much more successful. As a means of supplementing my teacher salary, I accepted a part-time job selling the World Book Encyclopedia. I was excited about selling the World Book because it had, in my opinion, the best testimonial a salesman could ask for. It was the only encyclopedia in the school library that was always worn out; the kids used it.

The World Book sales manager taught me an opening statement that was almost irresistible: "Mrs. Johnson? Bobby's mother. I am Mr. Evered, one of the teachers in Bobby's school. I'm also selling the World Book Encyclopedia because I believe in it and I know it can have a direct bearing on Bobby's education. If you would grant me just thirty minutes to show you how it can help, I will leave the final decision up to you, yes or no--okay?"

Now, I'll grant you, I had an advantage, being one of the teachers in Bobby's school. But there was no subterfuge; I always laid it all on the table and it was all up front. I am thoroughly convinced, however, that a nonteacher would have no trouble in gaining entry with a similar opening statement. I've often thought that an excellent opening statement would be, "Mrs. Johnson? Bobby's mother? I'm Mr. Evered; I represent the World Book Encyclopedia. Would you be kind enough to grant me thirty minutes to explain why the kids at school continually wear this set out, and to explain why the kids who have it at home can always finish their reference work? If you will, you can see the positive impact it can have on Bobby's grades. I will leave the final decision up to you, yes or no. Okay?"

By now you should see that careful planning is a must in selling. There is no substitute for knowing exactly what you are doing every step of the way. It's not a matter of playing the odds but a matter of turning the odds in your favor. When you know exactly what you are doing, the odds will always be in your favor. Knowing your customer, knowing the kind of results he seeks, knowing how your product or service will produce those results, knowing how to validate your statements, and knowing which techniques will be most persuasive are all part of selling. Professional salespeople have a firm grasp of this entire process. That is why they are professionals and successful. Following the RSVP selling process can bring you to a higher degree of professionalism.

9

Telephone Selling

The telephone is one of the greatest sales tools ever invented, if not *the* greatest. But the telephone is just that, a tool, nothing more. It does not replace the use of personal, face-to-face selling and it will never replace the ingenuity of the individual salesperson, but it plays a major role in modern selling. With today's high fuel costs, telephone selling is being used to reduce the sales/expense ratio in most companies. Travel is being curtailed out of necessity. Smaller accounts are being handled largely, if not entirely, by telephone. The necessity of getting firm commitments for sales appointments is becoming increasingly important, not only to avoid wasted selling time, but also to reduce travel costs to a minimum.

It has often been said that it takes a completely different kind of salesperson to sell by telephone, as opposed to the one who sells face to face. Experience, however, shows this to be untrue. Granted, there are some restrictive factors in telephone selling and there are some additional skills that need to be developed. But any good salesperson can learn to sell effectively on the telephone.

As telephone selling became a necessity for many companies, it was quite common to hear salesmen say, "It will never work for me. I've got to have direct contact with my customers." They were apprehensive about changing their style, but in time they found their productivity rising steadily. It required adjusting to some new and challenging situations and developing the necessary skills.

Historically, salespeople have wasted countless hours in waiting to see customers. Many articles have been written about how this waiting time could be used productively, for example, handling correspondence, studying product literature, and mentally rehearsing the sales message. Even though they obtain firm commitments for appointments, salespeople still find they must wait. At times they will be with a prospective buyer when a telephone call comes through to him. Some have seen the buyer purchase from a competitor over the telephone in their presence.

Two immediate advantages to telephone selling are that a lot of waiting time can be eliminated and travel time and expense can be reduced. A salesman or saleswoman can contact ten customers by telephone in the time it would take to drive to one. And today's buyers are accepting telephone selling as a way of life. These buyers are just as conscious of sales/cost ratios as are salesmen and saleswomen. And customers find that less of their time is wasted over the telephone. Salespeople consume more time when selling face to face, and buyers know it.

Since telephone selling allows us to eliminate most wasted selling time, it's only smart that we make the best use of it. Here are some ideas that will help you be successful at telephone selling.

Play the odds. The number of orders you write will be in direct proportion to the number of solid selling calls you complete. Your batting average (sales/call ratio) may not be quite as high, but you will come up to bat many more times and that will produce a greater number of hits.

When you're hot, keep dialing. Remember, you are closest

to your next sale right after you successfully close one. Don't stop for coffee to celebrate your successful sale; keep rolling while you're hot. Analyze and complete your detail work after you have finished your sales calls, but dial for dollars while you have the momentum. Coffee may cost only forty-five cents a cup, but it might be costing you fifteen dollars an hour.

When you're flat, stop! If you find you have no pep, no enthusiasm, and things aren't going well, stop dialing. Do something to get your motor running again. Lean back, relax, think through your last successful sale, and recall the excitement you felt when it closed. What made it successful? What did you say? Take a good look at your product. Is there a new, fresh way to present it? Try a new approach.

Maintain control. Be sure you have control of the sales interview and of yourself. Constantly check for customer reactions. Use questions to test the customer's attention and interest. Good communication is a two-way conversation and good salespeople are outstanding listeners. They have an important goal in mind: *listening* for buying signals and constantly working toward the close. Get the order now. Then get another, and another, and another. Keep selling until the customer stops buying.

Project sincerity. Learn to project a personality that expresses warm friendliness, sincerity, and a genuine interest in the customer's problems. Show confidence in yourself, your product, and your company. Show an enthusiastic love of your profession; it's contagious.

Set daily goals. Set sales goals every day and do whatever is necessary to meet them. Your productivity will be in direct proportion to your determination to meet your own (not your sales manager's) goals. Set your goals high. Nothing worthwhile was ever accomplished from a mediocre objective. The great producers have always been the consistent producers.

Get tuned up. The human vocal cords are the greatest instrument ever created, so use them as a professional musician uses his instrument. Every emotion can be projected through vocal manipulation. You can project happiness, sorrow, appreciation, excitement, sincerity, confidence, urgency, disappointment, and friendliness. Not to develop this valuable talent is a great waste. One of the best ways to develop the ability to project emotions is by reading aloud. Tape record as you read and then listen to the tape. Can you recognize the emotions? Practice, practice, practice.

Slow down. Effective telephone communication requires slightly slower speed than ordinary conversation. Why? Because your customer doesn't have the advantage of gestures, body language, and facial expressions to help interpret what is being said. Effective telephone speech should be around 140 words per minute, as opposed to normal conversation of 225 words per minute. Slow down, and you will be understood.

Speak in technicolor. Good telephone salespeople can vividly describe a spiral staircase in the dark. They could walk a customer up and down without missing a step. This may sound a bit of an exaggeration, but that's what telephone selling is all about, the ability to describe in such a way that your customer can see it perfectly. Many salespeople rely heavily on *power words* to get their message across, and the effective use of power words is essential to telephone selling. Power words amplify the customer's perceived value of the product. They help the customer *sense* a greater value in the product. They make the product worth more in the customer's mind. Consider the impact of these power words in describing your product to a customer:

rugged	lively	resourceful
sturdy	bold	honorable
solid	rich	unique
durable	elegant	ideal
enduring	stylish	outstanding
interlocking	charming	planned
rigid	bright	spacious
engineered	distinctive	desirable

impregnable	fashionable	inviting
striking	dynamic	uncluttered
exciting	honest	refreshing
lovely	fair	crafted
warm	respected	precise
cool	stable	dependable
sparkling	progressive	protected
comfortable	reliable	individualized
authentic	sound	guaranteed
natural	classic	healthy

Use sales aids. One of the greatest advantages of telephone selling is the ability to lay your entire plan in front of you; your customer can't even see it. You can even write particular statements or phrases you want to use and place them in front of you. You can write some strong closing statements so they are at your fingertips when you are ready for them. I know one salesman who had a spiral-bound directory of answers to almost every objection. As the customer stated an objection, the salesman lifted the appropriate tab for that objection—and there was the answer.

Plan every move. Telephone selling requires every bit as much planning as face-to-face selling, a fact many salespeople fail to recognize. Although as much planning is required, it is easy. Here are some tips that will make your telephone selling run a lot smoother:

1. Clear your desk completely, except for the items that will be used during the sales call. It is important to avoid distractions. Have the desk well lighted, see that the room temperature is slightly cool, and keep the office door closed.

2. Every day, without fail, have a call sheet made out with all customers or prospects listed in order of priority. If it is best to call certain customers at certain hours of the day, include them at the appropriate spot on the call sheet, each identified with the proper call time. It is best to complete tomorrow's call sheet at the end of today's business.

3. Establish your daily sales objectives, not in number of calls, but in terms of units, dollars, cases, and so on. There is nothing wrong in establishing call objectives (number of calls) unless a preoccupation with numbers of calls becomes a distraction from your selling efforts. One productive call is worth more than a dozen hurried and ineffective ones. Don't stop selling until your daily objective is met. And don't stop then—keep selling.

4. Have your sales plan well prepared. Before starting your calls, go through a brief checklist: Have I decided which sales approach I will use today? Have I picked out the primary features I plan to discuss? Have I decided which customer results I plan to discuss? Have I anticipated all objections and prepared answers for each? Which closing statements will I use? Do I have all sales aids laid out for easy reference?

5. In order to get warmed up, make your first call on a relatively easy account. If, however, your first call bombs out, don't let it make you gun-shy about making other calls. Just shake it off and keep calling.

6. Maintain a positive and optimistic attitude from the first call to the last. Just say to yourself, "These people are going to buy today; they are going to buy from me; and they will be better off because they did."

7. Keep your voice fine tuned to reflect enthusiasm and optimism.

8. Be certain that your opening statement will give your customer a strong desire to hear your complete message. Open up with a valuable result your product will provide the customer. Never, never, never open with "How's business?" or "How's the weather down there?" These are open invitations to a gripe session and can start the entire interview on a negative note.

9. Don't stop selling until the customer stops buying. Always ask, "Is there anything further?" Don't get so elated over one order that you hang up on the next six.

10. Post-call analysis is important, whether the sale closed

or not. What did I do right? What went wrong? How can I strengthen it?

11. Plan tomorrow's work and get today's detail work out of the way. Be sure everything has been properly handled so you can get a fresh start tomorrow. Part of your planning should include a few minutes in quiet meditation as you consider a new, fresh approach to selling that might be more effective. Is there a new way to excite your customer, a new way to describe your product, a unique opening statement?

12. Close your day with this thought: "My sales objective will always be the same; that is, to see that today's sales are better than yesterday's and worse than tomorrow's.

10

Prospecting

It has often been said that salespeople drive by more business than they get. To a large extent this is true because they lack organization in their prospecting efforts. Some concentrate their efforts on larger accounts and overlook smaller ones that could, collectively, produce a lot of sales volume. Lack of imagination is another reason a lot of business is missed. I have heard salesmen complain about having a bad territory when the only problem was disorganized salespeople. There usually will be more prospects for your product than you will ever be able to contact. But with some careful planning and a little imagination you will be able to wring maximum sales from almost any sales territory.

Any person who could use or resell your product is a potential customer. It is simply a matter of determining who they are and where they are, and then making contact. Just to give you some idea of the scope of potential business, take a few minutes to slowly thumb through the Yellow Pages of your telephone directory. With your own product in mind, ask yourself as you look at the ads, "Could these people either use my product or resell it at a profit?" You will probably find scores of potential buyers by this method.

It would be ridiculous to say that everyone is a potential buyer for your product. Certain products, of course, are limited to specialized fields and certain buyers. Diagnostic hospital equipment, for example, is limited to hospitals, clinics, and certain physicians. Many other products are similarly limited, for example, forklift trucks, technical equipment, oil well drilling equipment, and so forth. Regardless of the product you sell, however, you will certainly find many potential customers in your territory who are not buying from you. They will be buying from your competitors. Why shouldn't they buy from you? And don't say it's because your competitor has a lower price than you have. If that were a logical reason, then why isn't your competitor getting *all* of the business?

As you develop your strategy for prospecting, always aim for a fair share of the market, and the only fair share is 100 percent. Don't go after *some* of the business; go after *all* of it. If your present customers have reason to buy from you, there is no reason that others shouldn't.

SOURCES OF PROSPECTS

As mentioned earlier, a little time spent with the Yellow Pages will turn up several potential customers. Just keep in mind, "Who could use it or resell it at a profit?"

Your present customers may be able to refer you to others, especially if they are not in direct competition with each other. Referral business is especially important in the consumer market. A satisfied customer is usually happy to mention friends or relatives who could use your product. Never fail to ask a satisfied customer for several referrals. However, get permission to use your customer's name as you contact those referrals. Not only is it a common courtesy but it makes further contacts more meaningful. I have found that insurance agents are particularly adept at gaining referrals. When I have purchased insurance, rarely have I had an agent fail to ask me, "Do you know of someone else who may need this same protection?" If I feel better with the protection, why shouldn't others?

Many salesmen find it advantageous to belong to one or two civic organizations. It provides contact with potential buyers who in turn may refer you to others. The same is true for church groups, PTA's, professional organizations, bowling leagues, country clubs, and various other organizations. Your prospecting results will be in direct proportion to the number of people you contact. The product you sell will dictate the kinds of groups that will provide the greatest potential for business.

Your local newspaper, too, can provide some excellent leads. The engagement notices, for example, are of particular interest to several groups of salespeople. A couple about to get married will have additional needs for insurance and housing. With today's soaring housing costs, these engagement notices are of particular interest to dealers who sell manufactured housing, the only affordable housing available to many young married couples.

If your product is one that is sold door to door, then behind every door is a potential customer. With a strong and results-oriented opening statement, coupled with a reliable product and a professional sales interview, your potential sales volume is practically unlimited. It is an advantage to know the homeowner's name before you ring the doorbell, too. Many names appear on mailboxes. In most towns and cities, directories are available that list names. During your contact, be sure to ask for the names of neighbors. Always ask for referrals after a successful sale.

I once knew a salesman who sold customized stationery and business cards. Every time he found a convention of any kind in a hotel, he would go to the registration desk of the convention group and try to get a copy of the registration list. Surprisingly enough, he was usually successful, although I question just how ethically he got the list at times. Nevertheless, it provided him enormous listings of potential buyers. The local registrants were contacted in person, and others, by mail. Don't overlook this potential source of prospects.

State registration lists may provide prospects, too. Automobile registration lists are available in most areas. You may be able to get new homeowner listings from utility companies. Newcomer clubs and the Welcome Wagon may provide some productive leads. It is possible that a registration list from a local bowling tournament could give you some leads.

With a little imagination, you can find countless sources of prospects. Usually, wherever people gather there are some prime prospects among them.

For some reason, most retail businessmen feel no need for a vigorous prospecting program. They rely on advertising, promotions, and window displays to attract customers. Advertising and display are important, but a personal prospecting program could bring in a lot more business. When was the last time you had a retail businessman actually *ask* you to do business with him? Has it *ever* happened? Have you ever had a hardware dealer, for example, say, "John, spring is just around the corner. When you get ready for garden tools and fertilizer, I'd sure like to show you what I've got"? That's prospecting! Why don't more retailers do it? Business usually goes where it's invited and stays where it's appreciated.

Sales locators are used quite extensively in automobile, real estate, manufactured housing, recreational vehicle sales, and other high-ticket items. According to some state laws, certain types of "finder's fees" are illegal, that is, paying a fee to someone who sends you a customer who buys. Before using someone as a sales locator, check your state laws regarding legality. In most instances it is perfectly legal and ethical. Incidentally, I prefer to use the term *sales locator* rather than the common term *bird dog*.

If you use sales locators, give them some helpful instructions first. Tell them the types of people you are looking for, that is, qualified buyers, not just bodies. Give your locators a little sales information about your product so they will know what to say. Provide them with product brochures, if available, and have some referral cards printed for their use. Periodically, get together with your locators to discuss product changes or any other information that would be helpful to them. Give the locator some suggestions on what to say to people and where to find prospects. And by all means, when you complete a sale to a referred customer, pay the finder's fee promptly. Think of the volume of business you could gain if you had several people working as sales locators.

Wholesalers and retailers should get every single employee involved in prospecting. Any employee who draws a wage from the business has a vested interest in the income of the business and a responsibility to produce a portion of that income. That includes the stock clerk, the bookkeeper, the janitor, and the night watchman—every person on the payroll. Each of these employees should be asked regularly, "How much business have you brought in recently?" This responsibility for producing business should be thoroughly understood at the time of employment. It is not the responsibility of these employees to do the selling; that's the job of the salespeople. But it is part of their responsibility to bring in prospects for the salespeople to talk to. If I were a retailer or wholesaler, I would fire any employee who was not trying to bring in more income for the business. If you, as a salesman, call on retailers or wholesalers, you should encourage them to put such a prospecting system into practice.

The employees, just like sales locators, need some information to help them in their prospecting. Teach them how, tell them what to say, tell them where to look for prospects. Every employee should be provided professionally printed business cards for use in prospecting. For heaven's sake, don't print all the cards with a blank space for the employee to write in his or her name. That looks cheap because it is cheap. It makes a cheap impression. It doesn't cost much to print business cards and a few extra sales will more than pay for them.

Here are some suggestions for using those business cards. Pass them out freely. The more you get your name before the public, the better. Give them to your mailman, the barber, the hairdresser, the supermarket cashier, your physician, and nearly everyone with whom you come in contact.

At the end of the month, when you sit down to write checks to pay your monthly bills, enclose a business card in each envelope to be mailed locally. That young lady who opens the statements for Sears, Roebuck and Co. just might be a potential buyer, or may know of someone who is. Don't limit such mailings to one single month; keep it up for at least a year. Many employees open those statements. The more you get your name before them, the better. My business card goes into every single envelope in which my check goes.

Several years ago, the oil company for which I was working devised a highly successful promotion very similar to this. Every employee was provided a supply of cards to insert in all monthly mailings for six months. The card stated simply, "I enjoy doing business with you and I'd appreciate your doing business with me by buying products made by my company" (company logo was included). The effort was a complete success and those cards showed up at service stations by the thousands. Again, business goes where it is invited, so start inviting.

A fact you must face is that not all business is profitable. Some prospects don't offer enough potential to be worth the effort. Time should not be wasted on marginally profitable accounts when the time spent elsewhere would be more productive. The eighty-twenty rule states that 80 percent of the business comes from 20 percent of the customers. Prospecting efforts should be concentrated on those of higher potential. Low or marginal profit accounts could possibly be handled by telephone, allowing you to concentrate personal time on greater potential volume. Your product, your territory, and your time limitations will dictate where your prospecting efforts should be directed.

If a prospect doesn't buy, don't give up. Persistence pays off. If the prospect is worth going after once, he's worth going after again, and again. It is a good idea to assign account priorities, too, on prospects. You may wish to classify them as A, B, or C, with the A prospects those offering the greatest potential. The A prospects should be contacted more frequently, and always in person. You may limit your C prospects to telephone contacts only, and the B prospects will be some of each, depending on your time allocation and travel distance.

Always maintain a prospect file. Keep records of contacts, information gained, customer attitudes, and any information that will strengthen your next contact. Establish the date for your next contact and follow up religiously. Even though a prospect is happy with his present supplier, you may contact him some day when he is upset with the supplier and ready to make a change. It happens quite frequently, and the salesperson who maintains the contact is the one who usually picks up the account. Don't leave it up to the prospect to contact you when he is ready to make a change. You stay in contact with him regularly. It will pay dividends.

Centers of Influence

For certain types of products and services, certain people in town are in a position to lead you to more business. Bankers, for example, know when people are going into (or out of) business. They also know who are the most stable and successful businessmen and those who are continually growing and expanding. They know the most stable building contractors, jobbers, distributors, retailers, and professionals in town. Check with the local banks and the savings and loan associations. Tell them you are looking for a strong local businessman to represent your product and ask for a recommendation. Don't say, "You can't get that kind of information from a banker." I have done it time and time again, and so have thousands of successful salespeople.

The specific centers of influence will vary, of course, according to the product you sell. During my college years, I took a job with a local distributor, selling Catholic Bibles door to door. As a Protestant, I knew I would have to find the centers of influence if I was to be successful. There were two sales in particular I knew I needed to make in order to gain access to centers of influence—the local Catholic priest and the Catholic mortician. I succeeded in both cases and was able to gain referrals from each. My approach to the priest was, "Father, who in your parish is most in need of this kind of spiritual strengthening?" He was glad to refer me to some of the weaker people in the flock, and told me to be sure to tell them he sent me. There was something in it for him, for the wayward flock, and for me. That's good business. Some people will take issue with me and say that as a Protestant, I had no right selling Catholic Bibles. I disagree. I don't think you have to have a baby in order to be an obstetrician.

By the way, I *almost* sold the Catholic mortician a large quantity of Bibles. I nearly convinced him it would be a boost to his business to provide a Catholic Bible to every bereaved family he served. I still think it would have been a fine gesture. He had an objection, however, that stopped me in my neophyte foot tracks. He said, "I'm the only Catholic mortician in town and I already have all the Catholic business." I wasn't thinking fast enough to realize I could have sold him some Protestant Bibles to increase his trade. It didn't occur to me that my distributor handled both.

Regarding the Bibles, my other source of prospecting was the local newspaper's birth notices. Every time a Catholic baby was born, I would contact the parents the next day. They were always in the maternity ward at St. John's Hospital. That was a great center of influence—until the sisters ran me out.

Another mortician I know in Oklahoma is one of the best prospectors I have ever known. He maintained public contact through a newspaper clipping service. This was a few years ago when it was considered unethical for a mortician to advertise in any really aggressive way. Articles about local people were clipped from the newspaper, laminated in plastic, and mailed to the individual or family concerned. The only advertising involved was a notice on the back of the laminated article, "Compliments of (name) Funeral Home."

The mortician well understands people's motives. Everyone likes to see his or her name in print, and he provides a keepsake that will last forever. He is also a great source of sales for the newspaper, I might add. If a picture, for instance, of a local Little League baseball team of twenty youngsters appears in the paper, within a week, all twenty families have a laminated picture of the group, compliments of the mortician.

By the way, if you are one who sells to a retailer, you might pass this idea on to him as a successful promotional suggestion. It might gain some business for him with very little cost or effort. Think what this idea would be worth to a person who sells plastic laminating materials or equipment.

Another center of influence might be a situation or an occurrence, rather than a person. Here is one of the finest I have heard. A friend of mine has a father who retired in his sixties and learned to sell to supplement his income and to keep him busy. Now in his nineties, he is actively selling fire extinguishers in Texas. A residential fire is his prime center of influence. He immediately begins a door-to-door campaign of the entire neighborhood before the embers cool. Exploitation? No, it's good salesmanship.

Many situations become centers of influence and open enormous opportunities for sales. Think what rising fuel costs have done for small-car sales, to say nothing of sales opportunities for more efficient heaters, insulation, storm doors and windows, and caulking materials. Rising crime rates generate sales of alarm systems, locks, dead bolts, and weapons.

A local college or university can become a great center of influence for businessmen who want to go after extra sales. I recall a local service station dealer who attended a meeting of my fraternity to present his proposition. He asked that we identify ourselves as members of the fraternity every time we made a purchase at his station, so he could provide us a sales slip from the transaction. He said, "At the end of each month, bring in the stack of sales slips; I'll add them up and write the fraternity a check for 5 percent of the total."

That dealer became our sole source of funds for fraternity beer parties. When our sorority girl friends needed gasoline, oil, or other service station products, we would take the car in for them. When my parents' car needed tires, they were bought at that station. Nearly any retailer could gain business this way. It's just another method of prospecting.

Another center of influence may be an exhibition, a trade show, or a trade association. Nearly every industry is affiliated with a trade association of some type. The association may have local chapters. These include professional groups of every kind: doctors, lawyers, dentists, home builders, truck stop owners, office products dealers, real estate developers, petroleum and pharmaceuticals companies, training professionals, sales and marketing executives, hardware dealers, to name just a few.

Prospects? They are out there if you go looking for them. A little detective work on your part, a little thinking, and a little imagination can bring you a lot of extra business. You just have to go after it. As you seek new business of any kind, ask yourself three questions: Who could use my product? Who could resell my product at a profit? Where can I locate these people? When you find the answers to these three questions, go after the prospects.

I close this chapter on prospecting with a little poem that has been with me for years, author unknown:

> Just sittin' and wishin'
>   Ain't gonna change your fate.
> The Lord provides the fishin',
>   But you gotta dig the bait.

Happy diggin'!

11

Planning
the
Sales Call

Planning the sales call is one of the disciplines of selling I seriously doubt you have considered in more than a cursory manner. I make the statement out of experience, because I have found that the vast majority of salespeople neglect sales planning to a great extent. Some think it isn't necessary. Others are just too lazy to plan. Still others seem to rely on divine guidance to carry them through a sales interview. Regardless of their reasons, this neglect is one of their most costly mistakes.

In time, after you have gained a lot of sales experience, planning will take very little of your time. Until you have gained that experience, you would do well to discipline yourself to write sales plans on a regular basis. Most top-producing salespeople write sales plans as a matter of course. They learned the value of this discipline years ago.

Actually writing a sales plan forces you mentally to organize your material; it forces you to think ahead, to anticipate, and to learn. If you have thought everything through, organized it, written it, and seen it, you will be going into the sales situation much better prepared and more capable than if you play it by the seat of the pants. Your odds of succeeding will be substantially improved.

You will recall that the basic concept of RSVP selling is to answer four logical questions in the customer's mind in sequence:

R (Results) "What's in it for me?"
S (Source) "What's going to give it to me?"
V (Verification) "How do I know it will?"
P (Persuasion) "What should I do?"

Preparing a sales plan ahead of time will make it easier for you to keep your selling on target and to answer these four questions. Don't rely on your wits to carry you through a sales interview; plan every move carefully. I strongly recommend that you *write* each sales plan completely until you have gained enough sales experience to organize a plan mentally. Actually, I recommend that sales plans always be written, but I am not naive enough to think you will do it throughout your career. As you gain confidence you will probably begin to feel that sales plans are unnecessary. I hope you never make that mistake.

An excellent sales plan to use is shown in Figure 10. Have a local printer prepare it for you in pad form. It is possible that you might prefer to modify the form to suit your particular sales job.

Planning a sale goes beyond just thinking about it. It requires the careful development of a predetermined course of action you will take to reach the final objective, the sale. It must include the what, when, where, why, who, and how of getting the job done. It is laying out a predetermined course for the RSVP sales process.

There is a big difference between a "canned" sales interview and a "planned" one. A canned sales interview may be satisfactory in some rare cases, but our primary objective here is to develop a planned procedure that will result in more sales. Until you have gained a great amount of experience,

Figure 10. Sales plan form.

SALES PLAN

FIRM _____ PERSON TO CONTACT _____ _____

TYPE OF BUSINESS _____ COMPETITORS _____

PURPOSE OF THIS CALL _____

_____

MY OPENING STATEMENT ___ _____

_____

_____

FACT-FINDING QUESTIONS I WILL ASK _____

_____

_____

_____

(R) SPECIFIC RESULTS MY PRODUCT WILL PRODUCE FOR MY CUSTOMER _____

_____

_____

_____

_____

(S) SOURCE OF THE RESULTS (PRODUCT FEATURES WHICH WILL PRODUCE THE RESULTS) _____

_____

_____

_____

_____

(V) PROOF MATERIAL I WILL USE TO VERIFY MY CLAIMS _____

_____

_____

_____

(P) PERSUASION — CLOSING STATEMENTS I WILL USE:

1. _____

2. _____

3. _____

4. _____

5. _____

OBJECTIONS I EXPECT:

1. _____

2. _____

3. _____

4. _____

5. _____

6. _____

HOW I PLAN TO ANSWER EACH:

1. _____
   _____

2. _____
   _____

3. _____
   _____

4. _____
   _____

5. _____
   _____

6. _____
   _____

KEY POINTS I WILL USE TO SUMMARIZE _____
_____
_____
_____
_____
_____

you will find it wise to write each sales plan, study it, and then review it just prior to the interview. With time and experience, planning each sales call will become automatic. Salespeople who carefully plan each interview make more sales.

Let me explain the difference between a *canned* interview and a *planned* interview. If I write it and you memorize it, it's canned. There is, however, a place for a canned sales interview (actually, it will be a *presentation* rather than an interview). A canned presentation is usually used by a neophyte salesman when training time is unavailable. It's a matter of "memorize it and regurgitate it in front of the customer, and some of them will buy." The only other justifiable use of a canned presentation is in the case of the hard-headed, undisciplined salesman who refuses to use proper selling techniques and is not producing satisfactory results; his sales manager says, "You are going to say it this way, or you're fired!" Believe me, I often recommend that a sales manager take this stance, although I am basically opposed to a canned presentation.

A planned interview is something else. If *you* plan the material, *you* write it, and *you* memorize it, it's not canned—it's planned. You should memorize *your* opening statements, *your* answers to objections, *your* closing statements. That's planning. Whether you have memorized it or not, since it is *your* material, you have a great amount of flexibility during the interview, flexibility that is impossible in a canned presentation.

The sales plan form is basically self-explanatory; however, the various sections deserve some emphasis and discussion if your sales interview is to get the job done right. Basically, this concerns *what* you plan to do and *how* you plan to do it.

Heading

In preparing the heading of the sales plan, be sure the person to contact is the right one. Be sure he is the one who can either make or authorize the purchase. It is futile to conduct a lengthy sales interview with a person in the business who is not in a position to control the buying. The person who actually makes the purchase may be a sales manager, a service manager, a purchasing agent, an office manager, or the owner. Be sure you have the right person.

Be certain each sales call has a specific purpose. A professional salesman never makes a sales call just because he "happened to be in the neighborhood." Think how insignificant this makes the customer look and feel. Each sales call is made for a definite reason. Be sure you know exactly what you plan to sell before you contact the customer. Make each customer feel that he is the most important man in the world to you during the sales interview. Let the customer know that it is *his* business you want, that he is a specific target. Let him know that you *planned* this call for the sole purpose of seeing him or talking to him, and that right now nothing else is important.

In planning the specific purpose of your call, list the principal objectives you have in mind. What do you plan to sell? How many? How soon?

Although the next item on the sales plan form is your opening statement, you will prepare it *last*. After you have mentally organized the entire plan is the time to decide which opening statement would be most appropriate. The title of a book is decided after the author has completed the manuscript. Preparation of the opening statement will be discussed later.

Fact-Finding Questions

Chapter 3, "Determining Target Results," covered various questioning techniques, and I suggest a review at this time. Questions uncover customer attitudes, likes, dislikes, prejudices, biases, interests, and other data. Questions gain information that will give you an advantage in the selling situation. Use open-ended questions that encourage the customer to talk. In determining the questions you plan to pose, ask yourself, "If I could learn anything about this customer that would give me an advantage during the interview, what would I want to know?" Then go after the information. List at least five or six pertinent questions that would give you some helpful information.

Specific Results for the Customer

You have a reason for making this sale. What is the customer's reason for making the purchase? Unless the product will provide a result (value) for the customer, he isn't going to buy. This is where the salesman must ask himself a vital question, "Why *should* the customer buy?"

Perhaps your customer is planning to expand his business, add some new facilities, add more retail outlets, or remodel existing facilities. His obvious need here is for additional capital through increased profits. Perhaps you have an additional line of merchandise that will help him build profits. The customer's needs may be a reduction in inventory items, reduced operating costs, better product availability, better freight arrangements, smaller packaging, larger packaging, less chance of breakage, better adjustment policies, greater promotional support, greater public recognition and acceptance, or any number of personal or professional requirements. Remember, if your product or plan doesn't fit the customer's need, you will be wasting your time and his. You now begin to see the importance of knowing everything you possibly can about each customer. Only then are you really able to tie your selling techniques to his specific needs. You must know the kinds of results the customer wants and the kinds of results your product can provide for him.

Keep in mind that the results for one type of customer are not necessarily the same as those for another type of customer. For example, the expected results of an upholstered, steel-framed, swivel office chair would not be the same for a secretary who will use the chair as they would for the purchasing agent who might buy the chair for the secretary. The secretary would be interested in comfort, contour, reduced fatigue, appearance, adjustability, and safety. The purchasing agent would be more concerned with durability, ease of cleaning, and guarantee. Be sure your product features and results are directly related to your specific customer.

Source of the Results

Time will never allow you to present every single feature of your product. The customer will never have time or patience to listen to all. You must select those primary features that will produce the most impressive results and stress them heavily. But be absolutely certain to translate every one of the features you select into the expected results for the customer. The customer is not as concerned with the features as with the results he will get from them. You may find it necessary to modify your material during the sales interview. If your fact-finding questions indicate a different direction in customer interest than you had anticipated, you will find it necessary to stress those features that are in tune with his interest. That's called sales flexibility, and eventually it will become second nature for you. This flexibility is possible with a *planned* sales interview, but it is next to impossible if you are giving a *canned* presentation.

Proof Material

You must be able to prove any claims you make about your product. List any materials you plan to use such as cutaway models, booklets, pamphlets, specifications, testimonials, product samples, guarantees, photographs, periodicals, demonstration materials or equipment, references, laboratory data, advertising materials, statistical reports, and so forth.

Closing Statements

If you plan fewer than five closing statements, you are making a mistake. It would be better to memorize no fewer than ten and to use no fewer than seven. Remember, as stated earlier, the average sale closes on the seventh attempt. If you want to play the odds, never stop short of seven.

Don't devote your valuable time to preparing and conducting a sales interview, no matter how good it may be, unless you are going to ask for the prospect's business. His business is what you are after, and he isn't going to give it to you unless you ask for it. Sure, there are exceptions to this, but you will never earn a living by selling only to those customers who *offer* you their business. You have to go after it and ask for it. If you ask, usually you'll get it.

Before you write the closing statements you plan to use, review Chapter 6, "Persuasion." Select the closing statement you believe will be most effective. If that one doesn't work, write the second best, then the third, and keep writing until you have no fewer than five. Don't be afraid to ask for the business in no uncertain terms. Lay it on the table and hit it with a hammer. Leave no doubt in the customer's mind that you are asking for his business. You have done the selling job, you are entitled to ask for the business, so do it. The customer expects you to ask for it, so don't disappoint him.

Objections and Answers

Objections indicate interest, so welcome them. They give you an opportunity to point out more results. As discussed earlier, objections can generally be anticipated and you can prepare for them. Put yourself in the customer's place and determine all the barriers you might bring up *against* your proposition. You must remember that your customer doesn't know as much about your product as you do (or he'd be using it), so he will probably have several objections. He will continue to raise objections until he sees sufficient value in your product to warrant a purchase.

Any objection raised must be answered satisfactorily before you can close the sale. Plan at least one, preferably two, answers to each of the objections you list. It is better to plan ahead than to rely on your wits to carry you through the customer's objections.

Key Points to Summarize

Remember the sales scale? The customer is going to weigh the total value he perceives in your proposition against the price he will have to pay. As you present your product features and the results they will produce for your customer, you are adding value to the right side of the scale. But those results don't stay on the scale. As the customer becomes distracted, the value falls off the scale and hits the floor. Just before closing, you must pick up the best and put them back in his mind, get him thinking about them and aware of them. Otherwise, they will weigh nothing as far as your sale is concerned. At this point in planning your sale, you must decide on the basis of your experience which ones are most valuable. These are the results you plan to remind him of just before closing.

You will have to play this by the seat of the pants to some

degree. Which are the results to which he reacted most favorably during the interview? In which ones did he show the most interest? These you will have to decide during the interview. But be sure to use a good strong summary just before closing. It adds value where it is important—total perceived value in the customer's mind.

The Opening Statement

The opening statement is the last item on the sales plan to be completed. Before writing it, however, review the "traffic cop opening" (Chapter 4). Just imagine that the customer will say, "Stop right there! You have exactly one minute to tell me why I should listen to you." If your opening statement doesn't answer that question, rewrite it until it does.

A Final Word

I sincerely hope that the writing of sales plans becomes as important to you as the concepts of a results-oriented sales interview. It will always pay dividends. Review your sales plan just before you call on the customer. It will crystallize all the major points in your mind and immeasurably improve your odds of closing. Any top-producing, professional salesman will verify this.

Sales plans have served me well in other ways, too. When I have had proposals to present to my own management, I have been far more successful when I took the time to write a sales plan, considering the results my proposal would produce for the company, anticipating the objections management might raise, planning how I would overcome each, and planning a strong opening statement backed up with proof material. Careful planning has made it possible for me to gain approval on many major projects. Many were approved in the midst of heavy corporate cutbacks, economic crises, production layoffs, and belt tightening, although some required considerable funding. There is no question about it, salesmanship pays off, and it pays off best when it is well planned—in writing.

12

Retail Selling

At this point, let's separate the clerk from the salesman. I'm speaking of the in-store clerk whose vocabulary is usually limited to "May I help you?" and "Will that be cash or charge?" Some even extend their effort further with, "Will there be anything else?" It is an insult to the profession to consider such mediocre efforts as selling. But these clerks could be salesmen and saleswomen if they so desired.

I have talked to scores of clerks to determine why they make no effort to sell more. Their basic attitude is, "Why should I? I won't make any more money for it. There's nothing in it for me." Is it any wonder that clerks continually complain about their low wages? At their present level of effort, they're not worth more. It doesn't take a lot of talent to operate a cash register, make out sales slips, and sack the merchandise.

Nothing in it for them? Hogwash! There's plenty in it for them if they would only realize it. Managers and owners of retail outlets are always looking for the bright and ambitious employee to promote, and it will invariably be the one who produces more and is willing to put out more effort. Learning to sell may open the door to more profitable sales opportunities. It may lead to owning your own business someday. Managers of retail outlets usually advanced through the sales ranks. There is plenty of opportunity for the person with ambition.

CROSS SELLING

Rarely does a customer enter a retail store completely aware of all his or her needs. When was the last time you went to a supermarket, for example, and purchased only what was written on your grocery list? When was the last time you went to a hardware store for a single item and purchased only that item? When was the last time you went to a drugstore to pick up a prescription and purchased no more? Your own buying habits prove that cross selling is possible almost always.

In all probability, however, the additional items you purchased were prompted by something other than salesmanship. It's what's called impulse buying and was caused by the retailer's merchandising skill rather than salesmanship. That retailer knows how to display merchandise to get your attention and get you to buy on impulse.

Consider the supermarket, for example. Have you ever noticed how the staple items such as dairy products, produce, and meats are usually at the *rear* of the store? These staple items are the ones most frequently purchased. These items are stocked at the rear of the store so you will have to walk by other merchandise to get to them. That manager knows very well that you will be prompted to buy several items on impulse as you go by. You will also note that most impulse items will be displayed at eye level. The next time you go to the market note the location of such items as smoked oysters, flashlight batteries, film, highly advertised pet foods, pet supplies, shaving lotion, and miscellaneous housewares.

Other retailers are as adept at merchandising as supermarket managers. They display their merchandise in such a way as to take advantage of the traffic patterns. They literally force you to walk by the impulse items. This merchandising technique evolved from the basic idea that clerks won't sell.

The merchandise had to sell itself. What a waste of potential. The opportunities for cross selling are almost unlimited. Cross selling, sometimes called intensive selling, suggests further items the customer may want or need, things the customer might not have thought about. Cross selling is practiced widely in retail stores where the sales personnel are on commissions. An example is the salesman selling women's shoes. As soon as the customer has selected the shoes, the salesman suggests a matching or complementary handbag and then a belt. That's cross selling.

Think of the opportunities for cross selling in a sporting goods store. If the customer came in for a fishing reel, what would you suggest? Of course, a matching rod. Then what? A variety of lures, a tackle box, a reel case, perhaps additional spools of fishing line. The possibilities are almost unlimited.

If the customer purchased a camping tent, think of the possibilities for cross selling, including lanterns, camping furniture, camping stove, bedrolls, tent heater, ice chest, and so forth. Why pass up these possible sales when a mere suggestion could bring you additional sales?

Let me give you an example of what a little selling effort could do for you. About three years ago, a large local hardware dealer asked me to hold a two-hour sales seminar one evening for his sales personnel. I concentrated the entire meeting on cross selling. For every single item in the store I mentioned, the group named several related items to suggest to customers. The group worked up the following list:

Original Item	Related Items
Paint	Brushes, stirring rods, paint thinner, drop cloths, paint buckets, roller and pan, protective clothing, hats
Lawnmower	Gasoline can, air cleaners, trimming shears, hedge trimmer, fertilizer and spreader, insecticides, grass bags, grass bag holder

Original Item	Related Items
Hammer	Utility belt, nails, wrecking bar, other tools, toolbox, tool marking device, carpenter's apron
Charcoal Grill	Charcoal, starter fluid, barbecue tool set, utility table, food trays, electric charcoal starter
Antifreeze	Pressure radiator cap, hydrometer, radiator flush, stop-leak, drain pans

In addition to the related items, I suggested that each employee select one single item in the store each day to suggest to every customer, regardless of what the customer bought. I suggested that they select an item being featured in their current newspaper ads.

The dealer reported far better results than I had expected. Each employee was to keep a record of related items sold and a record of sales of the single daily item being mentioned to each customer. During the month following our sales seminar, the dealer reported sales increases of 14 percent as a direct result of cross selling. Fourteen percent of gross sales revenue was no small sum. He was able to reward employees with substantial bonuses.

The suggestions to the customers were always made in terms of results the customer could expect from the product. The salespeople were encouraged to tell each customer what the suggested product would do for the customer. If the suggested product, for example, was a long-handled dustpan, I discouraged such a question as, "Mrs. Jones, could I interest you in a long-handled dustpan?" After I discussed the sales scale and the RSVP selling process with the group, I suggested a professional style of selling: "Mrs. Jones, here is an item that can take a lot of the bending and stooping out of housework. When you sweep the kitchen, the garage, or front porch, just think how many times you have to stoop to pick up the dirt piles. With this long-handled dustpan you'll find the job a lot easier and a lot less tiring. Shall we add this to the new broom you just selected?"

I can think of no business in which it would not be possible to cross sell, using the RSVP selling process. The insurance agent can always sell additional coverages, such as home-owner's, life, fire, casualty, auto, and annuity policies. The service station dealer can always suggest additional services and accessories. The men's clothing salesman may suggest complementary attire, additional shirts, ties, belts, shoes, and socks. The liquor store salesman may suggest various wines, a wine rack, cocktail glasses, canned snacks, or a wine cooler. Even the pet grooming shop may suggest pet care items, new collars, doghouses, pet carriers, personalized name tags, leashes, or dog sweaters. The fireplace equipment shop may suggest glass fireplace doors, gas logs, a new grate, game room lamps, hanging baskets, a firewood rack, match holder, and various fireplace accessories. The local locksmith could suggest additional dead bolts, extra keys, peepholes, window locks, and complete alarm systems. Don't leave these potential sales to a display rack or counter. Go after them.

The possibilities for cross selling are limited only by your imagination. All you need to do is look around for the possibilities and start suggesting. These suggestions often do no more than remind a customer of things he needs but has forgotten. Consider, for instance, that worn-out, streaking windshield wiper blade. When it's raining, we won't stop to get it replaced. When it's not raining, we don't think about it. Think for a moment about the batteries in your flashlight. Just how fresh are they? What about the batteries in your smoke detectors? Do you have a saw that needs sharpening—if you had a file? That scratch on the dining room table you could repair, if you had a mark repair kit. Think about the antifreeze in your car that needs changing, that frayed fan belt that should be replaced, that oil change you forgot to get, that dashboard compass you have been wanting, or that extra rear-view mirror. Think of the loose leg on that dining room chair you would repair, if you had the glue and clamp for the job. Do you need to lay in a supply of furnace filters?

There are many things we need or want, but we rarely think of them at the right time. It takes a good cross-selling salesperson to remind us of them. It may mean a small purchase to you or me, but it can add up to a sizable sales volume for the astute salesman who suggests additional items to every customer. Make it a habit to suggest additional items to every customer you meet. You will be surprised how often it brings in extra sales.

SELLING UP

Selling up is closely related to cross selling, and they should go hand in hand. Why sell the $200 model if you can sell the $250 model? Why sell six pairs of socks if you can sell ten? Why sell quarts if you can sell gallons? Why sell the washer if you can sell the washer and dryer combination? Selling up means selling larger quantities, larger sizes, more sophisticated models, higher-priced items, or additional options above and beyond the basic product in which the customer was originally interested.

Granted, you may feel there is a question of ethics here, or you may feel that I am suggesting high-pressure tactics. Certainly not! It is a matter of judgment on the salesman's part. I would never suggest selling anything that is not within the financial reach of the customer. But if you feel the customer can afford it, would be happier with it, and would get better service from it, sell it!

Let me cite a perfect example of selling up that I encountered just last year. Now that both of our children are through college, working, and successful, I decided to indulge myself a little. I am an avid bass fisherman and decided to buy something I had craved for twenty years—a bass boat. I went to a local and reputable boat dealer and encountered one of the best salesmen I have ever met. We'll call him Jerry. I knew as much about buying boats as I did about brain surgery. I was rather conservative in my selection, looking for the bare minimum. I looked over the inventory, many of which were obviously beyond my means, and picked out one I thought would be satisfactory. At that point, Jerry turned on the salesmanship, and to this day I am grateful to him.

Jerry began with a series of questions. He started with, "Will you be doing most of your fishing alone?" When I said I wouldn't, he suggested that I think about seating space, walking space, and storage space.

Then he asked whether I would be fishing on the larger lakes in the area. When I said most of my fishing would be on the lakes, he said, "Jim, you'd better think about these sudden winds that come up on our lakes; you could get in trouble." He continued, "You would feel a lot safer in a little larger boat that is more stable and has a larger motor to get you to shore in a hurry." I agreed, and we began looking at some larger and more expensive models. As soon as we did, he started selling up. The conversation went something like this:

"As a bass fisherman, you'll want a model with front and rear swivel seats so you can turn to either side, won't you?"

"Yes."

"And you'll want an electric trolling motor that is powerful enough but quiet enough so it won't disturb the bass, right?"

"Oh sure."

"You'll want a model with a built-in live well to keep your fish in, too. You won't want to use a noisy stringer over the side where it can catch on brush and lose your fish. Besides, every time you want to move to a new fishing spot, you'll have to bring the stringer in so your fish won't drown, and that will get the bottom of the boat all wet. And you'll want the live well close to the front seat so you won't lose any time getting your lure back in the water, right?"

"You bet!"

"Jim, let me ask, do you take any beer or canned soft drinks when you go fishing?"

"Doesn't everyone?"

"Then you'll want a built-in ice chest right up there in front with you. That way you won't have a regular ice chest taking up floor space, and you won't have the lid blowing off while you're running across the lake, right?"

"Sure."

"And, Jim, fishing these deeper lakes, you'll want an electronic fish locator to help you find them. It also tells you the water depth, so you won't accidentally run the propeller into a gravel bar and tear up a $100 propeller."

"Gosh, yes!"

"And you'll need a waterproof storage compartment for your tools and supplies. And a rod cabinet to store the rods and reels in so you don't accidentally step on them and break them. And you can keep them under lock and key that way."

"Naturally."

"With the size motor you'll want, you will need a power tilt and trim on it so you don't have to manually lift that heavy motor when you're ready to trail it."

"I might as well go all the way, Jerry."

"Okay, Jim, right here is the one that's got everything *you* said you wanted. Do you want to arrange your own financing, or would you like me to handle it?"

"You might as well handle everything, Jerry."

Now that was salesmanship in its highest form. If Jerry had been one of those "may I help you?" clerks, he would have had a much smaller sale and I would have owned a boat that would, eventually, prove to be a disappointment to me. As a result of good salesmanship, he was happy, I was happy, and I'm still happy.

There was one statement Jerry made, however, that at the time I thought was an exaggeration. He said, "Jim, you'll catch more fish with this boat." But he was right. I do catch more fish, because I go fishing more often.

If you would look back through the dialog between Jerry and me, you'll see most of the elements of good salesmanship. He used every element of a professional sales process: results, source, verification, and persuasion. It was customer-results-oriented all the way. He constantly spoke in terms of what it would do for me. He asked questions. He verified information.

He suggested more and better things for me. He was selling up to a larger and better model I would enjoy more. He appealed to both reason and emotion. He even used a fine minor-choice question close. And I bought. Further, I might add, I spent about $2,000 more than I had anticipated. I refer all my friends to him, and if I ever decide to buy another boat, you can bet I'll go right back to Jerry, too.

The car salesman uses the same technique for selling up. He suggests the four-door model for greater convenience of getting in and out. He suggests additional options for greater comfort, convenience, and enjoyment, such as AM/FM stereo radio, 8-track stereo tape player, more luxurious upholstery, fancy wheel covers, CB radio, and many other options. He knows he will make more money and you will enjoy the car more.

The lawnmower salesman will suggest a twenty-one-inch model rather than the seventeen-inch model. It means you make fewer trips around the yard, finish the job faster, and have more time for your ball game on television (or to go bass fishing). He may suggest the rear-bagging model rather than the side bagger, so you can go between shrubs with it and have a lot less hand trimming to do. He will suggest a self-propelled model so you won't have to work so hard. That's selling up, and it means more enjoyment and less work for the customer.

The salesman who sells manufactured housing may suggest a larger model to meet the needs of your family. He may suggest a double-width model rather than a single-width model. This would nearly double the living space and may well be within the customer's financial limitations, especially when reduced to the down payment and monthly payment. The difference between the smaller model and the larger model may be far less than the customer expected. Then, too, the salesman may suggest various options, such as washer and dryer, frost-free refrigerator, carpeting, air conditioning, furniture, or built-in microwave oven.

The camera salesman has many opportunities for both cross selling and selling up. He will suggest various additional lenses, such as telephoto, zoom, wide-angle or close-up, various filters, flash units, and a carrying case. Above all, he will suggest a good supply of film and a book on modern photography.

The swimming pool supply company will offer a wide range of products and supplies, such as spas, floating lounges, saunas, pool furniture, testing kits, repair products, pool sweeps, cleaning brushes, and a variety of pool toys.

These illustrations are sufficient to trigger your thinking. Anyone selling in a retail outlet has countless opportunities to cross sell and to sell up. It is a matter of trying, that's all. Study your merchandise and you will think of many related items to suggest. Don't pass up sales opportunities when they come so easily. Remind your customers of items they may have forgotten. Each additional sale may seem small, but collectively they add up to big sales volume. Go after that volume.

If you are the manager or owner of the retail business, demand that your salespeople go after this volume, and teach them how to do it properly. When they get it, be sure they are paid something extra for it. They are worth it.

13

Additional
Selling
Tips

The list of ideas that would help you in selling is endless. Many have already been presented in this book. Some, however, don't seem to belong in any specific chapter. Therefore, I will devote this chapter to some tips that fall in a general category. Some of these ideas may seem more like advice than skills; nevertheless, they can help you become more professional.

PROFESSIONAL DEGENERATION

No matter what profession we are in, we all suffer professional degeneration to some degree. We grow tired of the routineness or repetitiveness of our work. We become discouraged from doing the same thing over and over again. We become tired of the same old presentation, the same demonstrations, the same objections, and the same problems, day in and day out.

So to combat this and to keep ourselves from going stale, we begin changing things. We try to find a different (not necessarily better) way of doing things. Before long we begin to realize we have slipped away from the fundamentals that made us productive originally. This problem exists not only for sales-people but for other professions as well.

I have observed this professional degeneration in sales-people by the thousands. I have observed degeneration in sales managers as well. I have seen managers stray so far away from fundamentals that they couldn't recognize a poor sales interview when they encountered it. I do not mean this as an indictment of the manager either. It is a common phenomenon throughout the human race.

I have accompanied sales managers on joint calls with their salespeople. After a call, I asked the manager, "What do you think of that salesman?" Even when the sales call was a complete atrocity from a skills standpoint, sales managers have made such glowing appraisals as, "He's great, he's dynamic, he does a fine job!" At that point I knew the manager had degenerated to the point that he could not recognize poor selling when he heard it. He could no longer differentiate between "dynamic delivery" and "meaningful content." He was impressed with the salesman's enthusiasm, his inspiration, his positive body language, his oratory, his flawless delivery—of *nothing*. The salesman was saying nothing, but he was saying it well. Basic selling skills were lacking throughout the interview. There was no real content. A dynamic delivery impresses, but the content does the selling. The manager was evaluating the wrong thing.

Don't misunderstand me. I am not saying that a dynamic and enthusiastic delivery should not be used. Of course, it is important, but only if it contains the basic skills that generate sales.

As you evaluate your own selling efforts, first evaluate from the standpoint of *content* and then, delivery. Master the content; then build a dynamic delivery. I have known highly successful salesmen who haven't smiled since 1949, never raise their voice in enthusiasm, never display an exciting gesture, but get the business. They have mastered the content. All the selling skills were present during the interview.

Analysis of Sales Interview

How, then, does one avoid this degeneration? It requires a disciplined effort on the part of the salesperson and manager. It means taking an objective look at *how* one sells. It means picking a sales interview apart, piece by piece, and identifying the specific selling skills that were present. Does it follow the correct selling process, that is, results, source, verification, and persuasion?

A cassette tape recorder is one of the best tools to use in analyzing a sales interview. Tape record one of your sales interviews and play it back for analysis later. But you will have to be absolutely honest and objective as you analyze your own work. As you listen to the interview on tape, write the answers to these questions, all of which are drawn from the material presented in this book:

1. Did I waste my time and the customer's time with excessive idle chatter?
2. Was the customer really *eager* to hear my message because of the opening statement, or was he simply *willing* to listen to me?
3. Did I talk primarily in terms of the *results* my product would provide the customer, or did I spend most of the time on product features? (Be honest.)
4. Did I probe with questions to uncover the customer's true needs, rather than assume that I knew what he needed?
5. Did I answer all objections to the customer's satisfaction?
6. Exactly how many *results* did I present?
7. Did I miss any customer buying signals?
8. Did I use strong, firm closes?
9. How many times did I actually try to close?
10. What am I going to do to strengthen my next sales interview?

You should make this kind of analysis after *every* sales

interview, whether you are new to selling or have been at it for years.

You can use other methods, too, to prevent professional degeneration. Attending a sales seminar will help put you back on a productive track. Reading a good book on salesmanship will do the same thing. As a professional salesperson, you should set a personal objective of reading no fewer than four books on salesmanship each year. Not only will they give you new selling ideas, but they will help you avoid the natural process of degeneration.

Ask your sales manager to accompany you on some calls, and follow each with an objective analysis. Just hope he hasn't degenerated too much to help you. Get a sales colleague to make some joint calls with you for the same purpose. You can prvide mutual evaluation. If you have a corporate sales trainer, ask him to make some joint calls with you. He is a professional at evaluating sales effectiveness.

Listen to cassette tapes that are marketed by experts in the field of selling. They provide many splendid ideas for evaluating your seling skills.

And last, but not least, ask a few of your own customers to tell you what they think. This could prove to be a real eye-opener for you. It takes courage to ask, but it may be your most objective evaluation. A customer knows what he wants in a salesperson and he can tell you if you've got it. Listen to him.

If your sales volume is decreasing, or if it is not increasing, don't be too quick to blame the territory, the economic conditions, the weather, or your high prices. Take a good hard look at your selling procedures. Use the questions I have given you to determine whether you have slipped off the track somewhat. If you have, put those basic skills back into your selling and you will see the results almost immediately.

KEEP THE CUSTOMER AGREEING WITH YOU
This could be construed as a manipulative skill, but it certainly helps strengthen your sales interview. It is slightly dif-

ferent from the concept of gaining customer agreement to your actual proposition. It is a matter of keeping the customer in an affirmative frame of mind throughout the entire sales interview. If you do that, you are much more likely to get an affirmative reply when you attempt to close. In a sense, the customer will have been *conditioned* to agree with you.

This technique has been used on you and me for years by professional salesmen, and in all probability you weren't even aware it was happening. Let me give you an illustration of how this technique works.

Several months ago I received a call from an encyclopedia salesman, asking for an appointment in my home. I usually grant such an appointment, not that I plan to buy anything, but I like to observe as many salespeople in action as I can. I learn from them. I will let almost any salesman in my front door if he looks safe and his timing isn't too inconvenient. I was particularly interested in this salesman because, as I mentioned before, I had once sold encyclopedias door to door.

The salesman had his books, charts, and brochures spread out on a coffee table and was beginning an obviously memorized presentation when he glanced up at our piano and saw a picture of our blonde, blue-eyed daughter. He asked, "Is *she* your daughter?" "Yes," I replied. He continued, "Isn't she a beautiful girl?" Naturally, I agreed with him—because she certainly is. "I'll bet you're proud of her, aren't you?" Again I said yes.

Here's the point I am making. That salesman couldn't care less about my daughter, but he made me agree with him *three* times. That's what he was after—agreement.

But he wasn't through with me yet. My wife stepped into the living room and asked if we wanted coffee. He immediately replied, "I'd love a cup of coffee, thanks." I am still convinced that he hated the stuff, but he was setting me up. My wife poured his coffee; he took a sip and said, "She certainly makes a great cup of coffee, doesn't she?" Of course, I said yes. And that yes is what he wanted, another agreement.

He continued. He glanced toward the window and we could both see that it was pouring down rain. He said, "Sure is raining tonight, isn't it?" Any darn fool could see that it was raining, so I agreed with him again.

He continued to intersperse his presentation with irrelevant questions to which he knew I would answer yes. These questions were carefully engineered in such a way as to avoid any no. He must have hit me with two dozen such questons. In addition, he used many questions regarding his product that would also elicit an obvious yes.

Here is why the technique works, especially on an untrained or unsuspecting customer. When the salesman gets to the end of his presentation, chances are I won't remember many of the specifics about his proposition. But I have a definite feeling (albeit subconscious) that "this guy has been *right* all evening; this must be a good deal"—and I sign the order. But I'm not smart enough to realize that 90 percent of the things I had agreed with had absolutely nothing to do with what he was selling. He was manipulating me into an affirmative frame of mind. He had me conditioned to agree.

He was also very careful never to ask me a question I could answer with a no. That could have been an obstacle to his sale. Had I given him a no during his presentation he would have had trouble in closing, because I would have remembered something negative somewhere during his presentation and I would be hesitant about buying. Chances are, I couldn't even remember what the disagreement was, but it would have fostered some doubt in my mind about his proposition and I would have objected immediately.

Having spent many years training salespeople, I was well aware of his questioning technique and was able to ignore his irrelevant questions, concentrating only on those pertinent to his product. But, I must admit, he was successful in gaining my agreement dozens of times during the interview. He had learned his lesson well, even though no sale resulted this time.

Keeping the customer in an affirmative frame of mind is a technique effectively used by insurance salesmen. During my short time in insurance sales years ago, I was provided a little pocket-size booklet of 100 questions to which the answer was yes. To answer any question in that book with a "no," you would have to be psychotic or someone who hated his family. We knew that the psychological arithmetic was there: the more times you could get the customer to say yes or nod his head in agreement, the more likely he would do it again when you asked him to sign the contract. He would have been well conditioned by the time of closing.

Getting a customer to say yes or to nod his head in agreement is extremely easy. When you ask the right question, smile, look him in the eye, and nod your head, the customer will react like Pavlov's dog and agree with you.

Let me give you a little insurance dialog here to show you how quickly you can get a series of affirmative replies from a buyer. Let's say I am selling an annuity type of policy to John Doe.

"John, you said you have worked for General Electric for fifteen years, didn't you?"

"Yes."

"GE is a good, strong company, too, isn't it?"

"Yes."

"It has a fine retirement plan too, doesn't it?"

"Yes."

"And you're going to look forward to retirement, aren't you?"

"Yes."

"At that point, you will be on a fixed income, won't you?"

"Yes."

"And inflation will continue to bite into it, won't it?"

"Yes."

"That would concern you, wouldn't it?"

"Yes."

"John, as a hedge against that inflation, wouldn't you like to have a guaranteed $300 a month on top of that GE retirement?"

"You're darn right."

And I'm not darn fool enough to ask him, "John, would you like to pay $80 a month the rest of your life to get it?" He'd probably reply with a blunt no.

Look what I just did to that prospect. In a matter of less than one minute, I got eight agreements from him. That is conditioning him to agree, and if I used a good positive close following a complete and affirmative interview I would probably have a sale.

Think how difficult it would be to say no to these questions an insurance salesman might pose:

"You are concerned about your family's welfare, aren't you?"

"You want your kids to get an education, don't you?"

"We read of tragedies every day in the paper, don't we?"

"Lightning could strike tomorrow, couldn't it?"

"Other drivers get careless, don't they?"

"Fire could strike without warning, couldn't it?"

"You want security while you sleep, don't you?"

"Wouldn't you like to avoid that worry?"

"It could happen to anyone, couldn't it?"

These are all conditioning questions, getting and keeping the customer in an affirmative frame of mind. Similar questions can be developed for any product or service on the market. This is precisely the technique I presented in Chapter 6 on "Persuasion," namely, the "three-question nail-down close." It is a rapid-fire conditioning for agreement before you close.

I question the ethics of using irrelevant conditioning questions such as those the encyclopedia salesman used regarding my daughter, the coffee, and the rain. I merely offer the technique because of its effectiveness.

I am sure you are already using many questions that are conditioners, for example, "Don't you agree?" "Isn't that right?" "Don't you feel that . . . ?" or "Isn't it important that . . . ?" Use such questions freely. Develop a long list of questions regarding your product that will condition your customer to agree with you. If you use them throughout your sales interview, you will find closing much easier.

ORGANIZE TO GAIN MORE TIME

A perpetual problem most of us face is the customer who grants insufficient time for us to conduct a meaningful interview. This is especially true for salesmen who call on purchasing agents or pharmaceuticals salesmen who call on physicians.

A purchasing agent has several sales representatives to see every day, in addition to his other duties. Consequently, he may limit sales interviews to ten or fifteen minutes. Often, a physician may limit a sales interview to five minutes between patients. Obviously, the salesman must use every precious minute wisely. It leaves no time for discussing the weather, the football game, or fishing conditions.

If, however, you are well organized and use the time wisely, you can usually get additional time. If you get your prospect sufficiently interested through a strong, results-oriented interview, he will usually grant the time you need. At least, you can get more time than other salesmen may get.

Several years ago a survey was conducted among a large group of purchasing agents to determine their likes and dislikes regarding sales representatives who called on them. The survey determined that purchasing agents granted an average of fifteen minutes per sales interview. Here is one of the questions posed in the survey: "If a salesman had an *organized* presentation (slide/tape, flip chart), would you be willing to grant him a longer appointment?" The reply was a resounding yes from 76 percent of those surveyed.

Just last year, a colleague of mine in the National Society of Sales Training Executives conducted a similar survey among purchasing agents to determine their feelings toward sales representatives who call on them. I think three significant complaints from purchasing agents will give you something to think about, because they are some of the very reasons appointments are usually limited to fifteen minutes or less. Purchasing agents have three main complaints about salesmen: they are disorganized, they waste the agent's time, and they don't know their own product well enough.

In an earlier chapter I mentioned a sales seminar I was asked to conduct for a major pharmaceuticals company. These salespeople call on both physicians and pharmacists. It is important to research a project like this in order to custom-build a meaningful and productive seminar. During a two-month period before the seminar, I contacted a large group of pharmacists and physicians to learn as much as I could regarding their relationships with pharmaceuticals sales representatives. Here are some of the major questions I asked each:

"How much time do you allow a salesman?"

"If he is well organized and makes a meaningful presentation, will you allow additional time?"

"What are your primary complaints about salesmen?"

"By what criteria do you select the salesman from whom you will buy (or whose product you will prescribe)?"

These interviews were real eye-openers for me and provided me some excellent ammunition for conducting a productive seminar. In almost every case, the physicians and pharmacists said they would grant additional time if the salesman was organized and was presenting something meaningful.

When asked about complaints, many of their answers ran in similar veins, that is, "They waste my time"; "They come in, check the sample cabinets, give me a brochure on a new drug, say they will check back later, and leave"; "Instead of telling me what I need to know, they leave a brochure and expect me to study it on my own. They don't realize that I haven't the time to do their job for them." Although these complaints were in the minority, they established a pattern.

The criterion by which physicians and pharmacists decide which product to accept, buy, or prescribe was fairly universal. That was, "It's the salesman who gets right down to business, gives me both the positives and negatives about his product, gives me enough information so I feel confident in using it, and is able to answer my questions."

My research turned up four major concerns physicians have regarding pharmaceuticals products, in order of priority:

1. Safety, for both the patient and the physician. In this day of malpractice suits, the physician has every right to be concerned for his own safety.
2. Effectiveness. Does it work? Does the patient recover faster? Does it bring relief?
3. Convenience. Will two injections (or doses) per day do the job, as opposed to four injections with another product? If so, less time is required for administration by the nurse, there is less discomfort for the patient, less chance for exposure to infection, and less frequent awakening of the patient.
4. Economy. Although economy was in fourth place, it seemed to be a concern to most physicians—economy for the patient more than for themselves.

It has often been said that a salesman's two most important assets are time and professional ability. Time is of no value if it isn't used wisely. Don't waste your time and don't waste your customer's time. Organize your sales interviews for maximum effectiveness. That may mean having an attractive flip chart prepared, a slide/tape presentation made, or a three-ring presentation binder prepared. Your company may already have such items available. If so, use them; if not, get some made. It's a good investment.

GET YOUR CUSTOMER INVOLVED

It was Cicero who said, "The sense of sight is the keenest of all senses." Therefore, in the interest of time and effectiveness, we must make our sales interviews more interesting and colorful by the use of visual aids. To the salesman who is sold on the merits of his proposition and familiar with every part of it, the interview may sound mighty convincing. The question is, is it as convincing to the customer as it is to the salesman? The effects of sight and touch are much more impressive and lasting than those of merely hearing. The prospect reacts more positively in the salesman's favor when he or she participates in the interview. Get the customer to look at the merchandise; get him to examine it; get him in on the act.

Psychologists tell us, and it is one of the basic rules of training, that people must be told something seven times before they will remember it. In a sales interview, time seldom permits such a practice. As a professional salesman, you can take a lesson from this and direct your efforts toward showing as well as telling.

But there is even more than showing and telling. Remember our objective, that is, to build the "total perceived value" in the customer's mind. To do so we must utilize every one of the customer's senses whenever possible. We must appeal to the senses of sight, smell, taste, hearing, and touch.

Customer involvement means his physical and emotional participation during the interview. We want him to think value, feel value, smell value, taste value, see value, and hear value. When he does, he will *perceive* value.

Customer involvement is, in essence, a role play with the customer. He is a part of the act; he is participating, both emotionally and physically. Demonstrating to a customer is not involving the customer. It is the difference between living through an experience and seeing it in a movie. It is the difference between making history and reading about history.

Providing physical involvement is putting the product in the customer's hand. Let him feel it, lift it, manipulate it, disassemble it, reassemble it, play with it. Get the customer to push buttons, pull drawers, pull levers, spin wheels, adjust valves—anything that gets him to do something physical.

Why does the sporting goods salesman hand you a rifle and say, "Feel that balance"? It is because we can "feel" more value; it puts our imagination to work; it mentally puts us out in the woods. That rifle is worth more to us at that moment than if it were in a sterile case, under glass, where we can't touch it. That's customer involvement. It creates desire and makes sales. Put your customer's imagination to work every minute of your selling. Keep him physically and emotionally involved every step of the way. Ask him to *do* something; ask him to *think* about something; ask him to *imagine* something. Involvement is a two-way role play.

The things you can ask a customer to do are limited only by your imagination. Consider the following as you think of ways to gain customer involvement with your product:

"Please open the doors to this dining room hutch and imagine how it will look with your fine china in it."

"Please read this short article from yesterday's paper regarding the rising costs of college tuition."

"Lie on this mattress and feel the comfortable support."

"Smell this cologne's fragrance and imagine your wife's reaction to it."

"Listen to the quiet running engine."

"Feel the surge of power as you accelerate."

"Taste a sample of this new pizza."

"Compare the weight of these two suitcases."

"Count the file compartments in this briefcase."

"See how quickly you can extract the square root of 20,736 on this electronic calculator."

"See how smoothly this pen writes."

"Take this pen and add up the savings we discuss."

"Jot down these outstanding features as we discuss them."

"See how easily you can remove that grass bag from the mower."

"Feel the fine texture of this material."

"Press this button and see how easily you can raise that heavy garage door."

"Press the test button and decide if you think this smoke alarm would awaken you."

"Slip this letter into the machine and count the vivid copies it makes in ten seconds."

"Try this cabinet drawer and see how quietly it glides on its nylon bearings.

"Feel how cool this dish is as you remove it from the microwave oven."

"Notice the delightful after-taste of this chablis wine."

"Feel the light weight of this aluminum ladder."

"Take this ruler and measure the thickness of that insulation."

"Just try to break the joint where we used this new glue."

"Take your shoes off and feel the luxurious depth of this carpet."

"Examine this piston taken from a test engine that used our oil for more than 50,000 miles."

"See how easily you can reset the time on this LCD watch."

"Read the label on this container and see what the product will do for you."

"Try it—you'll like it."

There is no end to the ways you can get your customer physically involved during a sales interview. It can be done with any tangible product, from the smelling of an exotic perfume to a test run on a fifty-ton piece of earth-moving equipment.

Use your customer's imagination to gain emotional involvement. This is particularly important when you are selling intangibles, but it works equally well with tangibles:

"Mrs. Jones, if this were your home, how would you arrange this family room?"

"Imagine your husband's reaction when he sees this."

"Imagine going down the highway, wind in your hair, fresh air sailing by, and the warm sun on your back as you ride this motorbike."

"Imagine powerful, toned muscles."

"Imagine your guests seeing this fine china on your table."

"Imagine the peace of mind you would have with. . . ."

"Imagine what would happen if. . . ."

"Imagine saving sixteen man-hours per week."

"Imagine how much more comfortable you would be with. . . ."

"Imagine what you could do with the savings."

"Imagine how your management will feel when this program succeeds."

The more your customer is involved, the more value he perceives in your product. Don't demonstrate; involve. Involvement is an important part of the RSVP selling process. It provides validation and persuasion and builds perceived value in the customer's mind.

I vividly recall a salesman who had me mentally involved from the beginning to the end of his sales interview. Several years ago, when our children were younger, we did a lot of camping. We had made a decision to buy a new tent. I visited three or four sporting goods stores to get some ideas. My shopping stopped, however, when I encountered a real professional salesman at Sears, Roebuck. The tent I was considering was eight by ten feet with a canvas floor and mesh-covered windows and door. Although he did a superb job of selling, I will mention only a couple of items to illustrate how he put my imagination to work.

When he pointed out the mesh-covered windows and door, what immediate thought came to my mind? Of course, it keeps the bugs out. But that salesman didn't even mention a bug. He said, "Mr. Evered, when you're out camping, you will never spend a night scratching." Do you see where he had me? Out in the woods in my imagination.

Nor did he use the word "ventilation." He said, "If you are out there some afternoon and the fish aren't biting, you can lie in this tent and read a book. And you won't have an old hot lantern in there either. You will have a nice cool breeze so you can really enjoy camping." That's salesmanship in its highest form.

When we discussed the size of the tent, he put my imagination to work again. He said, "When you go on a camping trip, you won't have to leave your kids at home, because this tent is large enough for all four of you. And if it startsto rain, there's enough room for all your camping gear inside. With this tent, when you get up in the morning, you'll never have to go outside into the bushes to put your pants on."

But I honestly believe he clinched his sale with one power word. As he pulled up the zipper on the mesh door of the tent, he looked my wife right in the eye and said, "Mrs. Evered, this one's *snakeproof*." She said, "We'll take it." With such involvement as that, how could we resist?

As you develop your own sales plan, build customer involvement into it. Think of every conceivable way you can get your customer involved, both emotionally and physically. It helps your customer sell himself.

PROJECT AN IMAGE OF CONFIDENCE

If there is anything in the world that is contagious, it's an attitude. Be enthusiastic and your customer will be enthusiastic. Be depressed and your customer will be depressed. Display doubt and your customer will doubt you. If you display confidence, your customer will feel confident.

An attitude is the frame of mind with which you approach a situation. Here you can understand the importance of knowing everything you possibly can about your product and about your customer. Couple that knowledge with valid selling skills and you have no reason to feel anything less than 100 percent confident. Sure, you are going to get turned down many times, but so what? Shake it off and keep going. Get rid of any negative thoughts you might harbor. They can't work for you, and they will certainly work against you.

As I mentioned in an earlier chapter, keep this thought uppermost in your mind before you approach each customer: "He's going to buy, he's going to buy today, he's going to buy from me, and he's going to be better off because he did." Drill that thought into your mind every time.

Have you ever noticed how many salesmen mentally go out of business during tough economic times? They convince themselves that business is bad and then set out to prove it. With such a depressed attitude, it is impossible for the salesman to conduct a really effective interview. As a result, sales go into a slump and he says, "See, I told you." It becomes a self-fulfilling prophecy.

Some businessmen mentally shut down in winter for some reason, especially in the manufactured housing industry. They are convinced that people stop buying in winter. The truth is, people don't stop buying; the salesmen stop selling. They cut back on advertising, cut back on their promotional activities, and reduce their sales force, the very things that will cause a business slump. When it comes, they also say, "See, I told you."

Don't ever let a defeatist attitude take over. No matter what the weather, no matter what the economic conditions, the goods have to keep moving, and it's the salesman who keeps them moving. A really good salesman will never draw a welfare check. Someone somewhere needs him. If you are good, you can sell under any circumstances. You just have to know you can.

Even when economic conditions or weather conditions are at their worst, never discuss it with a customer. As far as you are concerned, the economic conditions are always great and the weather couldn't be better. A good salesman never has a bad day.

I have not complained about the weather since the spring of 1973, and I have a cab driver in Atlanta, Georgia, to thank for it. It was the most perfect put-down I have ever had; I deserved it and shall never forget it.

I had just checked out of the hotel, headed for the airport, and was running late. It was cold, rainy, windy, and miserable outside. As I stepped into the cab, the driver tossed me the usual "Good morning" as he started out the driveway. I retorted with, "It's a lousy morning."

At that point the driver actually stopped the cab, spun around in his seat, pointed his finger at me, and said, "Young man, you and I were lucky enough to see another day. A lot of nice folks didn't make it through last night." I have not complained since. What a great attitude toward life. Just having another day makes it a great day. Think what such an attitude could do for any salesman. To this day, I have one stock answer when I'm asked, "How are you today?" "If I were any better I couldn't stand it." And I believe it.

There is more to positive thinking than most people realize. A positive mental attitude is one of the greatest assets a person can have, especially a salesman. A positive attitude is contagious, and every salesman should be trying to start an epidemic among all his customers.

When you are in the presence of a customer, stand or sit proud and erect, smile, beam with optimism, be the very portrait of self-confidence. Speak with enthusiasm. Enthusiasm is that unmistakable evidence that you are in love with your work and proud of your profession. This kind of posture and attitude will add immeasurably to your credibility with a customer. The pessimistic salesman thinks, "I've got to sell something." An optimistic salesman thinks, "I've got something to *sell*." An optimistic attitude and contagious enthusiasm will often outweigh a lack of selling skills. But if you have all of them, you're a sure winner.

KEEP LOOKING FOR A BETTER WAY

One of the chief marks I have observed in top-producing salesmen is the constant search for a better way of doing things—not just a different way but a better way. Unfortunately, there is no single way to sell. If there were, we could record it on tape and fire all salesmen.

What works well for one salesman may not work at all for

another. A skill that is highly successful for me may be a complete bomb for you. Every salesman must find those techniques that work best for him. The problem is, no one knows which ones are best for him. For every ten ideas you try, perhaps only one is successful on a regular basis under your conditions. But if you don't try all ten and give them a fair trial, you will never know which one is the winner. Failure to reach out for new ideas can lead a salesman into a career of stereotyped mediocrity.

I know many top-producing salesmen today who have been earning in six figures for years. The one universal quality among them is a constant search for a better way to sell, a better way to say it, a better way to demonstrate it, a better way to probe, a better way to answer an objection, a better way to get customer involvement, a better way to close. No single salesman knows the best way to close. He only knows what is working best for him at the present time. The successful salesman knows there is a better way, and he's always looking for it.

Herein lies the value in reading books on salesmanship and in attending sales training seminars. They expose you to scores of ideas to try. Out of them, certain ones will prove highly successful for you. Keep going back to the well.

But even as you find new ideas, it takes a disciplined effort on your part to put them into practice. You are perfectly normal, so you will resist change. It's easy to say, "One of these days I'll try this" and then put it in a drawer and forget it.

We all resist change because it is work; it is an imposition; it requires disciplined effort. Few people are willing to change without a fight. It is so much easier to stick with the old comfortable ways of doing things, ways that have produced results, have kept us on the payroll, have earned a living for us. So why change?

A salesman can do a masterful job of rationalizing his old way of doing things so as to avoid the strain of changing. It is this resistance that has allowed multitudes of salesmen to remain in the ranks of the "average." Sure, they stay on the payroll; they earn a pretty good living; and they are never quite bad enough to justify replacement, or quite good enough to be promoted. They really never produce the volume we know they are capable of producing. The situation eventually results in complacency. Don't let complacency rob you of an opportunity to improve. Develop an eagerness to find a better way. A truly successful man is marked by his constant desire to improve.

USE SALES AIDS TO THE MAXIMUM

Sales aids are designed to help you sell, but they won't sell a thing if they are in the trunk of your car, in a closet, warehouse, or stock room. Put these aids to use at every opportunity. These could be advertising reprints, point-of-purchase signs or banners, promotional brochures, "take one" brochures, floor plans, artist's renderings, display kits or racks, direct mail brochures, flyers, or many other items. Your company probably provides a host of such materials to boost sales. Use them.

If you call on retailers or wholesalers, you will usually find it necessary to help the customer install the materials, an additional service you can provide for him. They won't do any selling if they are in his stock room. Help him get them up before you leave.

Those of you who are retail businessmen well know the host of materials provided by or available through your suppliers. Take advantage of every one. These "silent salesmen" can stop a lot of shoppers if they are used in good taste. Keep the display materials and point-of-purchase items clean and neat at all times. Replace or remove them when they become soiled. If you use outside banner materials or strings of pennants, get them down as soon as they become weather-worn or frayed.

A WORD ABOUT RETAIL ADVERTISING

This book isn't designed to be an advertising manual, but advertising is an important part of your selling effort. Therefore, I am going to discuss one small segment of advertising that might help to strengthen your efforts. This section will discuss print advertising only, because that is the dominant medium used by most retailers. Most of the advice here will be equally pertinent to broadcast advertising.

A large portion of newspaper advertising is ineffective and a waste of money for three reasons. First is the retailer who has no one to turn to for professional help in developing effective ads. This is especially true in smaller towns.

Second is the retailer who insists on writing his own ads and does not have the specific expertise to do it right. Invariably, he will write the ad to impress himself but it fails to attract business. Most ads are written to impress the one who is paying for them.

Third are the media salespeople whose only interest is selling advertising time and space, with little concern for the results. One of their favorite tricks is to get you to put your own picture in your ad. This impresses your family, but you are buying no more than an ego trip. Your customers don't particularly care what you look like, and your picture isn't going to attract any appreciable amount of traffic to your business.

A few years ago I was conducting an advertising and merchandising seminar for a group of retailers in Phoenix, Arizona. One gentleman in the group had been a television advertising executive for twenty years. He said, "Jim, we have an iron-clad guaranteed method for getting a car dealer to advertise on our station fifty-two weeks out of the year." When I asked how he did it, he replied, "Just get him to do his own commercial." It's obvious who the better salesman is in this case. Unless you have the personality, the voice, and the countenance to appear as a professional on television or radio, leave it to the experts. For the next few days, notice the number of "do-it-yourselfers" on television, and judge for yourself.

What about professional help in developing effective newspaper advertising? There comes a time in the life of every businessman responsible for advertising expenditures when he at least considers getting professional help. Too often this is a fleeting idea, dismissed as impractical and too expensive. Yet, he may not be completely happy with his "do-it-yourself" ads or those conceived and executed by the media.

Fear of advertising professionals is commonplace, mostly because of lack of information about the business. A short "road map" through the maze may give you the confidence you seek and persuade you to seek professional help when necessary.

An advertising agency is a company in the business of promoting other companies' products and/or services for a mutually agreeable fee. Advertising agencies are usually divided into full-service and boutique types.

A full-service agency can usually offer services from conception of an idea to placement of the ad in the selected medium. Large full-service agencies may have a stable full of specialists, while the smaller ones double up in areas of expertise.

Boutiques come in many forms, but one of the more common is a creative staff from which the client may choose the services he wants. Many boutiques cannot, or do not, place ads for the client.

Combinations are common. In dealing with an agency, remember you need never buy the entire package, regardless of whether it is full-service or boutique. Do not hesistate to discuss budget with your agency people. They are businessmen, too, and fully understand the need to meet a budget.

Freelancers are to be found in every phase of the advertising industry—graphic artists, typesetters, logo designers, and so on. A good freelancer can save both time and money in the design and production of advertising materials. In addition, he or she may be more versatile than an agency. Remember, however, that his time is his money; he cannot afford to waste it in unproductive sessions. Many freelancers will charge for "planning sessions," especially if they believe their ideas will be used later by another person.

In dealing with any advertising professional, agency or freelancer, be brief and concise. If you do not have even a bare minimum of an idea, be prepared to pay for your artist's lost time and work when the concept is "not quite what you had in mind" and you did not give any definite instructions.

Money is the usual reason businessmen avoid professionals. The expense involved in producing a really nice piece of work may seem high, but a $50 ad that did not draw any business is not cheaper than a $100 ad that brought in $50 worth of business.

If budget is a prime concern, discuss it openly with your artist. He is used to working within strict money considerations. Once a bid is made, make him stick to it unless extraordinary circumstances warrant extra money. Extraordinary circumstances do not include underbidding to get the job and then jacking up the price to make a profit.

Established rapport between client and artist is of paramount importance. An artist cannot do his best work without the confidence of the client behind him. Once a good working rapport is established, it is foolish to change for the sake of a few dollars. The money may be important, but will the quality of the work be as good if you switch to a cheaper artist?

Regardless of whether or not you want professional help in most areas, one area almost demands a pro. Logo design is personal to the business involved and requires a strong sense of graphic design. Money invested in a good, strong logo will be returned many times in recognition and recall of your name.

Seeking professional help is nothing to fear. Your artist works for you, not for your newspaper, television station, or radio station. This alone should give you confidence in his desire to fill your advertising needs.

Selection of an agency or freelancer is usually done on the basis of such personal impressions as the way one shakes hands, the way one dresses, the way one combs one's hair. Because selection is so personal—personality conflicts between client and artist are deadly to any creativity—hard and fast rules cannot be set down.

Some factors to consider, however, are past performance in similar fields. But try to avoid the specialist in your specific field. He may have conflicting accounts. Ask present clients why they are doing business with him. Ask former clients why they are not. Try to analyze how effective his efforts have been for others. This is tricky because of the myriad factors that can affect advertising. In the end, however, you will have to depend on your own reactions concerning a particular artist or agency.

Finally, if you believe your advertising could be helped, seek a professional. But don't get an agency just because "everyone else has one." Neither of you will profit from the relationship in the end.

A final word about full-service agencies. You do not pay a premium price for the placement of the ad in the newspaper. The agency is paid by the newspaper for placing the ad. The agency usually can get a better rate than you can, and the agency fee still comes from the newspaper. They work in a manner comparable to that of a travel agency, which receives a fee from the airline, and you pay no more than if you had booked the flight yourself.

14

Guidelines
for
Success

Throughout my more than twenty years of training sales personnel, perhaps the most frequent question I hear is, "What makes a salesman successful?" It is also one of the most difficult to answer. There is no pat answer, there is no panacea for success, but there are some general guidelines that will help ensure a successful career in selling. All the selling skills included in this book are aimed in that direction. At this point I am going to discuss those things above and beyond selling skills that will contribute toward a successful career.

Every salesman and saleswoman, every manager, and every sales trainer will have his or her own set of rules or guidelines for success, and you may disagree with some of those I believe are most important. You may think I have omitted several specific ones that you feel are paramount. Be that as it may, I wish to share with you ten specific things that I believe are at the top of the list, on the basis of my observation of thousands of successful salesmen and saleswomen.

Rule Number One
Always use valid selling skills. Do what you know is right, regardless of what you may see or hear others do. If you are

convinced that the skills presented in this book are valid and will work for you, use them religiously. I will always suggest that you keep looking for better ways of selling, but use ideas and skills that have been validated on the firing line by successful salespeople. These are the skills I have shared with you by means of the RSVP model.

From time to time you will see and hear salesmen who seem to violate every rule in the book, sell by the seat of the pants, and ignore the skills taught by their managers or sales trainers. Don't let this sway you toward a comparable pattern. You do what you know is right; it will pay off for you in the long run.

Rule Number Two

Conduct yourself at all times like a professional. This includes your grooming, your attire, your manners, your dependability, and the way in which you treat others. Display pride in yourself, your company, your product, and your profession.

Take a genuine interest in others, especially your customers. Don't *act* interested; *be* interested. They are dependent upon you for many things. To a large degree you will have a direct effect on their success. If, through your efforts, customers are able to become more successful and prosperous, you will have made a significant contribution. They are dependent upon you for fresh ideas, better ways of doing things, innovations, and a wealth of information they can use to improve their very life-style. Being a professional salesperson is no small responsibility; never take that responsibility lightly.

One of the keys to being a professional is the ability to take an objective look at yourself, to be able to evaluate your own strengths and weaknesses. Perhaps this should begin with a personal application of this idea, that is, rating yourself against some set of standards. Following is a personal balance sheet

for you to use in rating yourself. Compare your assets against
your liabilities:

PERSONAL BALANCE SHEET

Assets	Liabilities
Personal:	(Opposite of the assets)
Physical health	Vices
Mental health	Character weaknesses:
Spiritual health	Intolerance
Financial health	Greed
Personality	Immorality
Appearance	Intemperence
Attitude	Prejudice
Education	Dishonesty
Ambition	Lack of ambition
	Lack of self-discipline
Professional:	Lack of open-mindedness
Knowledge of products	
Knowledge of marketing	
Knowledge of customers	
Knowledge of company	
Knowledge of self	
Skills and techniques	

It is extremely difficult to rate one's self against such standards, but it is a good idea to take an objective look at ourselves once in a while, to compare our assets and our liabilities to see what our "net worth" is—our net worth to ourselves, to our families, to our company, and to our profession.

The key to success is to capitalize on our strong points while
working to eliminate our weaknesses. You are the key to your
own success. Only you can develop the assets; only you can
correct your weaknesses. Self-analysis is a good starting point.
The ability to analyze yourself objectively and then do something about it is all part of being a professional businessman or
businesswoman.

Rule Number Three

Continue to grow in your job. There are three basic reasons for growing in your job. First is the pride in doing better and better. There is a great sense of achievement in doing a better job. Second is the financial reward it brings. The better you do, the more you make; a valid reason for continued growth. And the third reason for growing in the job is to prepare yourself for greater responsibilities. Never forget, the first prerequisite for promotion is excellence in the present job. There will always be greater opportunities for the person who is willing to go that extra mile. While you are on the present job, concentrate on excellence in that job. At the same time, study for the next step. Set yourself a career target and go after it.

I sincerely hope you are with a company that has a formal sales training program. Whether you are new to sales or have been selling for years, your company's sales training program can help launch you into one of the most exciting, enjoyable, and profitable careers known. Here you will gain the skills and knowledge required to do a really successful job. The training will, no doubt, be based on the successful experiences of other salespeople.

But a launching pad is all it will be. Throughout your sales career you will learn something new every day. Continuous training will be offered. Take advantage of every bit of it. Read books on salesmanship and marketing. You will learn from every one of them. You will continue to pick up ideas and techniques that will work for you and boost your earnings.

If you are a veteran in the sales profession, welcome the company's sales training program with open arms. The sales representative doesn't live who knows all the answers, including you and me. You need to learn the company's policies, its products, its distribution system, its problems, its programs, and its way of doing things. The training program is designed to do just that.

Your company's sales trainer may be the best friend you ever had. He can strengthen your future and have a direct bearing on the standard of living you will enjoy throughout your career. Your trainer's job is to help you be more productive. Chances are, the trainer has had years of experience in developing sales personnel. Take full advantage of it. It is your career. The trainer will do his part in teaching, but you must do your part in learning. Your career will be directly affected by how well you apply yourself in the training program.

In many companies the field sales manager trains the sales personnel. Often the manager is provided a company manual that guides the program to see that effective training takes place. At times the manager is left to his own devices to impart the knowledge and skills required to do the job. But training the sales personnel is the most important part of that manager's job.

If you are with a company that has no sales trainer, and the responsibility lies in the hands of your sales manager, let me give you a suggestion as a birthday gift for your manager. It is the finest book that has ever been written to help him train you. The title of the book is *The Sales Manager As a Trainer,* published in 1977 by Addison-Wesley Publishing Co., Inc. Edited by Jared Harrison, it was written by a group of the nation's most experienced professional trainers, all members of the National Society of Sales Training Executives. In my professional opinion the book is a must for any sales manager. Get it for him.

At the risk of sounding immodest, I would further recommend you give your manager a copy of my own *Shirt-Sleeves Management,* published in 1981 by the American Management Associations (AMACOM). It was written as a guide to building healthier and more productive supervisor-subordinate relationships in any work environment, including sales. It will help your manager work with you toward a positive career development plan.

In the majority of cases, that sales manager came right out of the ranks of the sales personnel and is thoroughly experienced in selling. The manager was probably promoted because of an impressive sales record. But that manager isn't necessarily a professional teacher. He was never trained to be a teacher. Selling and teaching others to sell are two entirely different sets of skills. So you may have to do a better job of learning than the manager does teaching.

Nonetheless, that manager has a genuine interest in bringing you to a productive level as quickly as possible. Pay attention, listen, practice, and follow the instructions the manager gives you. You may have to do a lot of the learning on your own. Take a lot of notes and practice all the techniques you're given. They work. That manager has a big stake in your success. Your success enhances his success.

The manager will probably begin the training by providing you a host of company materials, such as price sheets, product brochures, and so forth. Study them thoroughly and learn everything you can about the company, its products, how they are marketed, shipped, priced, and the like. It is possible you will spend some time in a factory or plant, learning how the product is manufactured. Or you may spend some time in a warehouse, learning the distribution system. Every one of these activities gives you valuable experience and information.

Eventually, the sales manager will have you accompany him on sales calls, to see how to apply the skills. You may also be assigned to travel with a seasoned sales representative for the same purpose. Listen and observe carefully.

Before making a sales call with the manager or the sales representative, discuss the objectives of the call, what is to be accomplished, what problems are anticipated, history of the buyer, and so forth. This will help give you a perspective on what you will be observing.

After each sales call, discuss what happened, regardless of whether the call resulted in a sale. What did you learn on the call that will help you on the next? In the evenings, while out of town, discuss the day's activities, the sales calls, territory planning and routing, and any necessary reports or correspondence that must be prepared.

After several trips observing others sell, you will get an opportunity to do things yourself, usually in the company of the salesman or the sales manager. Remember, do things the way you were taught. Before each call, discuss the objectives. After each call, welcome a "curbstone conference" with the manager. Let him tell you what you did well, where you could improve, and how you might have done something differently. Listen and make the necessary changes before making another call.

There is nothing more exciting than that sweet day of success when you close your first sale. It is a moment you will never forget, and it will come sooner than you think if you listen to your trainer.

Your company may have a corporate manager of sales training who provides additional skills training. If you are that fortunate, you will be able to grow to a productive level much faster. And the corporate trainer is a professional teacher, usually with a successful sales background as well. His full-time job is the professional development of sales representatives and sales managers. The training will provide you a concentration of learning and practice that will be extremely valuable to you. Here your training will be supplemented with the latest audio/visual aids and training materials, perhaps including closed circuit television equipment for practicing selling in a role-play situation. It gives you and the trainer a chance to replay the situation and discuss it for strengths and weaknesses. It is an extremely valuable training tool.

Your time in the company's centralized training program, under the direction of a professional trainer, will probably be the most valuable time you'll ever spend. It will have a strong influence on the kind of future you will enjoy. Take full advantage of it and welcome any further opportunity to return for some refresher or advanced training.

From the day you are hired until the day you retire, you will be receiving volumes of the company's printed materials and correspondence. Every piece of it serves an important purpose. Study all of it thoroughly, whether you are new on the job or have been with the company for years. If you do, you will be a more capable and informed individual and will be a more suitable candidate when a promotion into management is under consideration.

The same is true of correspondence and reports for which you are responsible. They all serve a useful purpose, and it is imperative that you develop a reputation for handling all correspondence and reports in a conscientious manner and on a timely basis. It's part of your job.

There is no substitute for practice. Some of the selling skills will come easy for you. Others will be a little harder to master. But the salesman who practices his presentations over and over again, and hones them to a fine edge, is the one who enjoys the highest degree of success. Set the pace early in your career, at the very outset of your training. Practice, practice, practice.

Practice on your family, practice in front of a mirror, practice as you shower before going to work. Practice just before calling on a buyer, and practice after calling on him. Make a cassette tape recording of your presentation and give it a critical analysis to see how it can be improved. Make the necessary changes and practice it again, using the recorder. Listen to your techniques as you travel to and from work. Listen before you go to bed at night. Analyze your selling techniques before going to sleep, and think about them again as you are getting ready to go to work the next day. Let this analysis become a regular part of your daily life; let it become a permanent habit. After you have been in sales work for a long time, it should still be an important part of your every day. Regular, critical analysis is one of the hallmarks of a truly professional salesperson. It separates the pros from the duffers. Only you know which you want to be.

And finally, as part of growing in your job, take every opportunity to attend sales meetings, seminars, college and university lectures. These will help you keep up to date on the latest concepts in the field of selling and marketing. Everything is in a constant state of change, and success comes to the salesperson who keeps up with those changes.

Rule Number Four

Maintain your balance of loyalty between your company and your customers. You will be serving two worlds of different values and you have a responsibility to each. Never compromise one at the expense of the other. As I mentioned in a previous chapter, there will be times when you will have to say no to a customer when he asks for something you cannot do for him. Don't be a buck passer and say, "I'll check with my sales manager." Take a firm but courteous stand and tell the customer no.

There will also be times when you have to fight with your management to get something for your customer when you know it is the right thing to do. If it's right, fight. If you will, recall the triangle I mentioned earlier, the triangle of the three principals in any sales transaction, that is, you, your company, and your customer. Each is entitled to a profit from the transaction. You are responsible to see that it is profitable for all three. Doing this means maintaining the balance of loyalty among the principals. None is more important than any of the others, yourself included. Imagine yourself coming in for a landing in a Boeing 727, and ask yourself, "Which of the three landing gears is most important?" The answer is obvious, none. You need all three for an effective landing. The same is true of the three principals in the sales triangle. You are the maintenance man for the triangle.

Rule Number Five

Develop a reputation for reliability. Make promises sparingly and keep them religiously. Keep appointments at all times. If you say you are going to be there, be there. Your customer isn't interested in the congested traffic, the bad weather, or your aunt Agatha's hernia operation. If you find it impossible to keep an appointment, call ahead and reschedule.

Reliability includes detailed follow-up work, too. If you tell a customer you will find out certain information for him, do it. If you say you will call back later in the afternoon, call back. If you tell him you will put something in the mail for him Thursday, mail it Thursday, not Friday. If you promise a shipping date, be sure it's shipped. If you quote a price, stick to it.

Rule Number Six

Support your company policies as if you had written them yourself. There will be times when you disagree with a policy, perhaps feel it is completely wrong. Just remember, the people in management who wrote the policy probably had a lot more information at hand than you and were better able to understand its impact on the entire organization. Many policies are established because of various legal constraints upon the business world, for example, truth in lending, truth in advertising, fair trade laws, and the Civil Rights Act. The roots of many corporate policies are to be found in the law.

However, don't be afraid to question a policy. Go to your supervisor and discuss how you feel. There is nothing wrong in that, but once a decision is made regarding one of your company's policies, stick to it. Remember, there is a reason for every policy, even if you don't know what it is.

Rule Number Seven

Always give your company a good day's work. As a salesman, you won't be working under time clock conditions as do factory workers. If you are out on a sales territory, there is no one to get you out of bed in the morning, out the door, and onto the territory. That is your responsibility. Never let your company wonder whether you are on the territory. They should know you are out there. This is part of your reputation for reliability.

Think of yourself as a one-man business. You have been contracted, in essence, to generate revenue for your company. You cannot generate revenue except when you are selling. When you are not selling, you are a cost factor. Granted, time between sales calls can and should be used productively, but when you are not selling, you generate costs. Think of yourself as being unemployed between sales. You are out of business the instant you complete a sale. You are back in business the minute you initiate your next sales interview. This perspective is important to any top sales producer.

From a practical and selfish standpoint, when you are at home, you are not producing any revenue for your company or for yourself. This excludes telephone selling, of course.

One of the worst traps a salesman can fall into is a series of rejections that make him demoralized so he leaves the territory as an escape from the rejections. I will say this, however, regarding becoming demoralized. It is far better to go home and talk it over with your spouse than to go to a bar and try to drink your troubles away. That has killed the careers of many salesmen.

Don't let a turndown be a slowdown. If you want a good, profitable career in selling, you will have to learn to take rejection without coming apart at the seams. It's part of the job and you might as well get used to it. No matter how carefully you plan, there's no 100 percent guarantee the customer will buy from you. You know that as well as I. Whatever the reason, accept the rejection gracefully, thank the prospect for the opportunity to see him, and start looking for another prospect.

Concentrate on your strengths, your ambitions, your capabilities, and your desire to help others. Think about them when you go to bed, when you get up, while at the dinner table. Keep these positive thoughts in your mind, and they will soon drive out all those negatives that work against you. If you can do that, you could have a great future in selling.

Rule Number Eight

Don't be satisfied with average performance. Earlier in the book I stated that an average salesperson is just as near the bottom as the top. Certain salespeople seem prone to remain buried in the ranks of the average performers. These people are rarely good enough to promote or bad enough to fire. This is unfortunate, both for the individuals and for their companies. The individual never enjoys more than average income, and the company is getting no more than average productivity.

Why, then, do they remain among the ranks of the average performers? Believe it or not, it's often voluntary. This is particularly true in an organization where sales personnel are on a straight salary with no commission or bonus. This kind of organization tends to attract "securecrats," the nongamblers. They enjoy the security of knowing exactly how much they will be paid each month. Rest assured, it may not be very much, but they can depend on it. The system fosters an attitude of, "Why should I work any harder? I won't be paid any more."

Under a security system, most salespeople have no desire to be at the top of the sales ranks for fear that increased quotas will require them to work just that much harder next year. They enjoy a cushion of unexpended ambition as long as they remain average. They are the least conspicuous people in the organization; they hide in the ranks.

Some remain in the average category because they have not yet mastered the proper selling skills and are doing nothing to correct the situation. They make little effort to improve. Rather than reaching out for better skills, they seem to keep doing the same things harder and harder, or doing the wrong things better and better. It is, in essence, a lack of ambition;

they are too lazy to try mastering more productive skills. They easily become complacent with their lot in life and don't want to disturb it. They complain about poor territories, their high-priced merchandise, lack of company support, poor economic conditions, and uncooperative customers. They rationalize their own mediocrity with every excuse in the book. The fault always lies elsewhere. Invariably, there will be a high turn-over among this group; they tend to look for a better territory, a better company, and so on. They are blind to their own incompetence. I place a great share of blame in this situation on the salesman's manager for allowing such mediocrity to continue.

Another factor that keeps certain salespeople in the ranks of the average is attitudinal, that is, the salesperson's attitude toward what he or she is doing for a living. There are, unfortunately, a lot of people in selling who think the profession is something less than prestigious. They are somewhat ashamed of what they do for a living. They display no pride in what they do. They harbor an erroneous concept of the job and seem to feel that you can make a living in sales if you can't do anything else.

This attitude has a direct and damaging effect on the person's ability to sell. He lacks self-confidence, lacks persistence, and approaches nearly every selling situation with a negative or defeatist attitude. Obviously, his productivity will forever remain average or less. He is a predestined failure.

Top-producing salespeople are self-motivated individuals. They have that quality of being able to keep going under any conditions. They are drivers, pushers, and producers.

A plaque in my office sums up the characteristics of a professional salesperson. It states:

There are three kinds of people in the world:
Rowboat people, who have to be pushed and shoved along to get anywhere.
Sailboat people, who keep moving when things are smooth and the wind is blowing them along.

Steamboat people, who keep going under full power and stay on course, regardless of conditions, wind direction, fog, or rough seas.

You have to make a choice of which kind of salesperson you want to be. You can be a steamboat salesperson if you want to be that self-motivated individual who keeps going under all conditions. The choice is yours.

It has often been said that all motivation is self-motivation. I think this is especially true of salespeople. When you are out there in the territory, there isn't always someone there to pat you on the back when you make that big sale. You face crises alone, you face rejection alone, you face problems alone. You spend evenings alone, facing the four walls of some motel room.

Let me give you what I think is one of the most important pieces of advice I could ever offer you: Learn to sustain yourself on less praise than you know you really deserve. A salesman is a highly competitive individual; he hates to lose; he thrives on winning; he savors recognition and achievement. By his very nature, he needs constant reassurance of his worth. But, by the very nature of his job, there isn't always someone there to give him that reassurance. This is one of the reasons I have always taught sales managers to stay in regular and frequent contact with their salesmen.*

As a professional salesperson, you may have to provide your own spark, your own fuel. But there is one great source of motivation that I recommend you use regularly. If you are married, stay in close contact with your spouse when you are on the territory. Call her (or him) no less than three times a week, every night if possible. I don't care how high your telephone bill gets. If your company won't pay the bill, pay it yourself. It's a good investment in morale. It can keep your spirits up so you can do a better job on the territory. It also fosters a healthier marriage.

* James F. Evered, *Shirt-Sleeves Management,* AMACOM, 1981.

When you call home, discuss your rejections, discuss your successes, discuss your problems—get it off your chest. Your spouse is one of the best sounding boards you can have, a great source of encouragement and motivation. Furthermore, this regular contact and communication is important to your marriage relationship. Believe me, your wife's job is as hard as, if not harder than, yours.

I had always said that my wife earned 50 percent of my salary, just staying home, taking care of the kids and the house. That is, until the time she was hospitalized for three weeks and I had to stay home and look after things. I was wrong; she earned 90 percent.

Be a self-motivator. Be proud of your successes, pat yourself on the back, reward yourself with a good steak dinner. *Know* you are good. Be concerned about your rejections but not worried. Analyze them to improve the next interview, but shake off the rejections. They are just a natural part of selling; accept them as such, no more.

Strive for excellence in the job. Develop that driving urge to excel in competition, to be the best. Accept no less.

Rule Number Nine

Develop a contagious enthusiasm for the importance of your goals. Man is a goal-oriented beast. Goals keep us driving ahead; they foster ambition; they give us something to work toward. When we reach our goals, we enjoy the thrill of achievement, whether personal or professional goals. Without goals, our work has no purpose.

Goals are important to your company, too, and you have a responsibility to make the maximum contribution toward your company's objectives. The organization will achieve its objectives only when the individuals within that organization reach or exceed their objectives, whether those individual objectives were dictated or mutually developed.

Never be satisfied with company objectives if you know you can exceed them. Don't be satisfied in just winning a race if you know you are capable of setting a new Olympic record. Go for the best. As a territory sales representative, you are responsible for wringing from that territory every possible ounce of business you can. Never be satisfied with less. The thrill of achievement is the greatest thrill of all.

Your personal goals are every bit as important as your work goals. Unfortunately, few people have ever established clear-cut personal goals; they don't really know what they want out of life. Sure, we all want to make more money, live in a better home, drive a bigger car, and so forth. But these are not really life goals. They are just healthy ambitions or wishes.

Few people are able to give a personal definition of the word *success*. They have never clearly established in their own minds what success really is. Could you define it? I doubt it. In your mind, is it money, prestige, status, standard of living? Unless you could complete the following sentence, you have not defined your own personal success values. "I would consider myself a complete success if. . . ." Could you complete it? Or try this one: "I would be perfectly satisfied if. . . ."

Perhaps your success value is money. If so, could you name a realistic figure? How much money? If it means a bigger or better home, describe it. If it means status, what would it look like?

It is not as easy to define success as one might think. That is why so few people are able to establish clear-cut definitions of what they want out of life, other than simply *more* of everything (but they don't know how much more).

Define your success values. Where and what do you want to be in two, five, or ten years? What specific thing do you want to achieve during that time? What do you want to accomplish, reach, produce, or gain?

Unless you have clearly defined your success values, there is no possible way you can concentrate all your efforts to produce the thing you want out of life. You will burn up the majority of your efforts in peripheral activities that will not contribute toward what you want. You must see every single day and what you do during that day as contributing directly toward something you want out of life. Unless you can see today as contributing directly toward one of your life goals, then you will be *spending* another day, rather than *investing* it. You will be living today just to get it out of the way so you can start another one just like it tomorrow. Don't waste your days in peripheral activities. Make each one move you closer to something you want out of life, but first you must define specifically what it is you want.

Once you have defined your life goals, develop that contagious enthusiasm for their importance, a commitment to achieve them. Then allow nothing to sway you from activities that will help you achieve them. Develop the persistence to stay in the race until you've won. Don't give up, keep driving ahead, knowing you can reach the top.

Without goals, life has no purpose. Without commitment, life has no excitement. Without persistence, you rob yourself of the thrill of achievement. Don't let this happen to you. You are worth more than that.

Rule Number Ten

Never compromise your reputation with poor-quality work. Your reputation is an evaluation of what others think of you: your management, customers, friends, colleagues, family, neighbors, and associates. Their evaluation of you can have a greater impact on your success than perhaps your evaluation of yourself. Self-esteem is extremely important, but the regard in which others hold you is equally important. There is a great element of interdependence involved in the success of any person's career. To put it simply, we all need each other; therefore, the impact others can have on our life must be considered. From a career standpoint, your reputation in the eyes of your management is one of the most significant. From a sales standpoint, your reputation in the eyes of your customers will have a direct effect upon your ability to produce and succeed. Following the suggestions I have presented in this book will help you develop a favorable reputation in the eyes of everyone.

The factors that contribute toward a favorable reputation are too numerous to mention here, but some of the most important include honesty, ambition, intelligence, persistence, commitment, concern for others, integrity, and a driving urge to be the best there is. Only you can develop these characteristics in yourself. Others can help, but in the final analysis none can be developed without your permission and your determination.

It takes a lot of work and dedication to build these qualities, but no one ever said that life was easy. Success comes to those who are willing to work for it; there's no such thing as a free lunch. Only you know how far you want to go, and only you know how much energy you are willing to expend to get there. Quality work is your vehicle to success. To compromise on the quality of your work will mean an equal compromise on the quality of your success. It's your choice.

But quality is not static. In order to sustain a high level of quality in your work, it will be necessary for you to continue to grow, to change, to learn, to study.

In selling, as in any profession, training is a never-ending process. In this modern world of fast living, everything is changing: customers, business, products, services, and everything related to them. Since professional salespeople are the key individuals who keep our economy on the move, they must keep abreast of all changes that affect their careers.

Products are continually improved, and the salesperson is the one who must translate these changes into the results they will produce for the customer.

The person who has the ability to keep up with these changes, the ability to determine the results they will produce, the ability to make others see the value in them, the ability to demonstrate, to explain, to show, and to be convincing, is truly a unique individual. These professional abilities, coupled with effective planning to gain productive selling time and with an oversupply of ambition, courage, determination, and enthusiasm, make those persons outstanding in today's business world. They are a special breed, set apart from the ordinary. They are professional salespeople, and the business world is not only dependent upon them, but proud of them.

Epilogue

It has often been argued that selling is 80 percent art and 20 percent science. Frankly, I cannot agree with this ratio, but it's a moot point. I think there is a far greater degree of predictability when valid techniques are followed. You can prove this point by observing the techniques of the top sales producers. They are disciplined beyond belief; they use valid skills; they have a reason for every move they make; and there is a definite repetitiveness in their patterns of influencing buyers. Sure, they are flexible and are able to alter course as the situation dictates, but that altered course will have been planned well in advance. These people know what they are doing every step of the way. They never fly by the seat of the pants.

Admittedly, there is a great degree of art in selling. Not every technique will work in every case. When you are dealing with human behavior and reactions anything can happen. But you can certainly plan ahead and be ready for the unexpected. The RSVP sales model can help you plot an effective course in any event. It gives you a road map to selling that keeps you on target at all times, even when a customer's behavior deviates from the expected.

Never lose sight of the fact that *results* are always your primary target in selling. The only purpose of selling is to produce results for the buyer. The only justifiable reason for buying is to gain results. The salesperson's job is to get the customer to perceive the results he or she will gain by buying. When he buys, the customer has gained, the salesman has gained, and the company has gained.

Whether you are the owner of a business or a salesman for someone else, your objective is to bring in as much revenue as possible. As a salesman, you are the revenue producer for your business, and the amount of volume you produce will be in direct proportion to the number of people you are able to influence. The number of people you are able to influence will be in direct proportion to the degree to which you follow valid selling techniques. It is a matter of self-discipline. The RSVP model has given you a proven path for developing that self-discipline.

When you are in a selling situation, follow the model every step of the way. Study the model over and over again. Reread every chapter until the material becomes an integral part of your life. Practice, practice, practice until every technique becomes a habit. But even as you learn, develop, and use the techniques presented, never stop looking for an even better way, a better technique of selling. Find those techniques that work best for you, with your personality, with your particular product, and with the people you will be facing.

There is a world full of people out there who need you and need your product or service. Those people are searching for results. Your product or service can produce those results, but nothing is going to happen until you tell them about it. That's what selling is all about. Remember, selling is not something you do *to* a person; selling is something you do *for* a person. As a salesperson, you are a problem solver, a results producer, one who *serves* others. If you can perceive selling in this light, you are well on your way to a successful career in selling.

In this book I have shared with you the best of the best.

Perhaps I should feel remiss that so little of what I have presented is original, but I do not. Throughout my sales career I have learned from many, the thousands of salesmen, saleswomen, sales managers, and sales trainers who have unselfishly shared with me. I have brought you the best they have had to offer.

My personal career has been highly successful because I have learned from others and have shared with others. From a professional standpoint, three groups in particular have had the greatest impact on my career. First are the truly professional salespeople I have known, those who shared successful techniques with me. Second are the many mediocre, unsuccessful, and unprofessional salespeople whom I have known. They have taught me the things to avoid and I have wholeheartedly condemned their shortcomings throughout this book so that you, too, might avoid them. The third group are my professional colleagues in the National Society of Sales Training Executives who, for the past seventeen years, have shared the very best in techniques for training sales personnel. These men and women are the cream of the crop in the sales training profession, representing the finest companies and industries throughout the United States and Canada. My association with these professionals enables me to share with you the very best in selling skills from such companies as 3M, Exxon, Du Pont, Reynolds Metals, Dresser Industries, Goodyear, Kaiser Aluminum, State Farm Insurance, Cessna Aircraft, Dr. Pepper, Merck and Co., Coca-Cola, Del Monte, Seven-Up, Carnation, and Uniroyal, to name only a small number of the companies represented in the society.

If you have learned from this book, if you have grown, you are to some degree indebted to this fine group of colleagues. They have contributed toward your successful career; I have merely been the vehicle. They would share my pride in having made a contribution to your success.

As you continue to build a productive career, follow the successful ideas presented in this book, follow the guidelines provided in each chapter. Follow the RSVP sales process at all times. These are all yours for the taking.

I will not wish you "good luck" in your career. A successful career is not built on luck. It is built on hard work, determination, open-mindedness, and a genuine concern for other people. The very best I can wish you is good selling!

Index

on impulse, 170–171
signals of, 77–79, 109–110, 134

call objectives, 147
calls, cold, 137–140
canned interviews, 160, 162–163
cards, business, 153–154
centers of influence, 155–158
choice close, minor, 113–114
Cicero, 189
civic organizations, 151
claims verification, *see* verification, claims
clerks, 50–51, 169–170
closed-end questions, 33–34
closing of sale, 76, 93, 108–109
buying signals and, 77–79
doubts of customer and, 79–80
"puppy dog" approach to, 73–74
rules for, 110–111
sales plan and, 166–167
techniques for, 112–122
timing of, 110
see also objections
cold calls, 137–140
competition
customer testimonials and, 68, 69
product knowledge gained from, 47
concession close, 114–115
confidence, in image of salesperson, 194–196
Confidential Account Diary, 126–130
consumer, *see* customer(s)
containers, product, 70
contractors, 98
courtesy, 59, 87
credibility, 66–67
cross selling, 170–174

customer(s)
affirmative conditioning of, 182–187
awareness of results by, 36–37
buying signals from, 77–79, 109–110, 134
closing of sale and, *see* closing of sale
doubts of, 79–80
emotion and logic in decisions of, 23–24, 39–43
experience of, as verification, 74–75
information about, salesperson's, 125–130, 135–136
involvement in sale of, 70–71, 190–194
name of, in interview, 33
objections of, *see* objections
personality of, *see* personality, customer
psychological needs of, *see* psychological needs
rapport with, 85–86
"reading" of, 25–27
referrals from, 150–151
reselling by, helping with, 136
in sales triangle, 124
as stallers, types of, 99–106
testimonials from, 68–69
for wholesale products, 55–57
see also buying; prospects

defensiveness in customers, 86
degeneration, professional, 179–182
demonstration, product, 70–71, 190–194
Depression, Great, 4
development, self, 5, 206–211
Diary, Confidential Account, 126–130